THE LITTLE BOOK OF

Roses

Jacques Barrau
Philippe Bonduel
André Ève

Flammarion

Q U E S T I O N S

From the royal gardens of ancient Persia to peasants' plots in China, from the grounds of private mansions to public parks, roses bloom eternal. Does this contradict Robert Herrick's warning to "Gather ye rosebuds while ye may"?

Roses still flourish in the wild. Yet most of the roses we encounter today, whether exquisitely complex or beautifully simple, are the product of centuries of natural and controlled crossbreeding. Are the roses at the florist's shop and the roses enjoyed today in public and private gardens the result of artistry, a passion for beauty, or laboratory work? What new forms can we expect to see in the future?

The sight of lovely burgeoning roses can take one's breath away. Are there special methods or secret techniques for growing roses successfully?

A N S W E R S

Orientation p. 6

The alphabetical entries have been classified according to the following categories. The categories are indicated with a small colored rectangle.

■ Botany: Types and classification

■ Cultivation: Techniques and care

■ History: Arts and culture

The information given in each entry, together with cross-references indicated by asterisks, enables the reader to explore the world of roses.

The Story of the Rose p. 10

The Story of the Rose provides a comprehensive overview of the themes and information provided in the alphabetical entries.

Alphabetical Guide p. 26

The entries tell you all you need to know to enter the universe of roses. They are enriched with detailed discussion of the main varieties of roses, historical information, and cultivation tips.

THE BIRTH OF THE ROSE

The Rose's Roots

Rose bushes continue to flourish in the wild throughout the northern hemisphere, producing unruly and prickly branches with handsome flowers. These are the direct ancestors of all species of domesticated roses, including the most elegant hybrids.

- *Botanical Definition*
- *Bourbon*
- *China*
- *Damask Roses*
- *Floribunda*
- *Gallica*
- *Hybridizing*
- *Mutation*
- *Polyantha*
- *Species*
- *Spontaneous Crossbreeds*
- *Wild Roses and Dog Roses*

The Ever-Evolving Rose

To reduce rose breeding to laboratory science and genetics would be to ignore the aesthetic and creative aspects of the pursuit. Like criteria for beauty in all realms, roses are constantly evolving, along with our appreciation for them.

- *Blue*
- *Bourbon*
- *English Roses*
- *Horticultural Classification*
- *Hybridizing*
- *Modern Roses*
- *Old Roses*
- *Old Versus New*
- *Perfume, Potions, and Potpourri*
- *Portland Roses*
- *Rambling Roses*

Breeding Roses

Although it was once solely the affair of amateur growers, creating and raising varieties of roses is now a multi-million-dollar industry.

- *Blue*
- *Breeding Roses*
- *English Roses*
- *Flower Shows*
- *Genetics: Making Luck Work*
- *Hybridizing*
- *The Name of the Rose*
- *Patenting*
- *Tea Roses*

GROWING ROSES

Ornamental . . . and More

What are roses for? The rose is beautiful to look at, but it has also been put to practical use almost as much as it has been idealized and associated with sensual pleasure.

- *Attar of Roses*
- *Bouquet*
- *Medicine*
- *Fragrance*
- *Perfume*

Seeds and Stock

For a long time, improving upon known plant stocks was a matter of chance as much as of experiment. Following the search for new plants, the establishment of botanical gardens concentrated on understanding and controlling rose evolution. Today, growers rely on developments in genetics.

- *Blue*
- *Genetics: Making Luck Work*
- *Hybridizing*
- *The Making of a Rose*
- *Mutation*
- *Sowing*
- *Spontaneous Crossbreeds*

Gardening Know-How

Raising roses is less difficult than you may imagine! All you need is common sense and a little knowledge. And there are countless books, magazines, and catalogues to help you along.

- *Care*
- *Cutting and Layering*
- *Disease*
- *Forcing*
- *Grafting Your Own Roses*
- *Harmony in the Garden*
- *Location*
- *New Roses and Old Bushes*
- *Old Versus New*
- *Planting*
- *Packing*
- *Replacement*

PHILOSOPHY AND THE GARDEN

Gardens of Eden

The rose and the garden have long inspired thinkers and theologians. In Persian, "garden" means "paradise," while in the Middle Ages, Christians and Muslims alike saw the garden as an ideal world, walled away from harsh realities.

- *Harmony in the Garden*
- *Medieval Gardens*
- *Medicine*
- *Persian Poetry*
- *Romaunt of the Rose*

A Passion for Collection and Creation

When botany was the domain of apothecaries and cooks, gardens were first and foremost for useful plants. With the discovery of the New World, however, they became living catalogues of rare and interesting plants, including the rose. Inevitably, the passion for collection evolved into the desire to create ever more varieties.

- *Flower Shows*
- *Gardens to Visit*
- *Harmony in the Garden*
- *Hybridizing*
- *Josephine, the Empress of Roses*
- *Medieval Gardens*

The Art of the Rose

Gardens delight our senses and touch our emotions. From Sissinghurst to Giverny, great gardens reveal the aesthetic sensibilities of their makers and their visitors alike. In these places the rose provides a delightful combination of color and scent.

- *Attar of Roses*
- *Beauty*
- *Bouquet*
- *Fragrance*
- *Harmony in the Garden*
- *Paintings*
- *Replacement*
- *Selecting Roses*

MORE THAN JUST A FLOWER

The Mystique of Roses

Rose symbolism covers both the sacred and the profane. Since antiquity, the rose has been associated with mystery and wisdom, and various roses have been the emblems of royal houses, secret societies, and military confederations.

- *Arthurian Legend: The Round Table and the Rose*
- *Compass Rose*
- *Crown of Roses*
- *Gather Ye Rosebuds While Ye May*
- *Josephine, the Empress of Roses*
- *Rosary*
- *Rose Window*
- *Secrecy*
- *War of the Roses*
- *White or Red?*
- *Yellow Rose of Texas*

Love in All Its Forms

O My Luve's like a red, red rose . . . The language of love has always been spoken with roses. From thorn to petal, from scent to texture, all parts of the rose communicate passion.

- *Beauty*
- *Love: A Language of Colors*
- *Romaunt of the Rose*
- *Rome*
- *White or Red?*
- *Yellow Rose of Texas*

Life and Death

Roses celebrate beauty, but beauty is fleeting and life always comes to an end. Poets have long used the rose to express this essential truth, and even children's games and popular songs have found the correlation irresistible.

- *Beauty*
- *Gather Ye Rosebuds While Ye May*
- *Persian Poetry*
- *Romaunt of the Rose*
- *Rome*
- *Rosary*
- *Rose Window*
- *White or Red?*

THE STORY OF THE ROSE

The rose has always been as full of mystique and meaning as it is of thorns. Because of its rounded shape and splendid colors and textures, it has taken myriad meanings, from purity to secrecy to the swiftness of life's passing. Its symbolism is often as complex and contradictory as the contrast between the white rose* and the red.

The rose grows easily and everywhere, and has thrived over the years through both spontaneous* and deliberate hybridizing,* as well as grafting.* Because its numerous varieties have been created out of plants from round the globe, some see the rose as a sign of an underlying harmony among the world's nations.

For the ancient Romans,* the rose was the flower of the gods. Today it illustrates the wonders of science and the recent progress in genetics.*

I. The Birth of the Rose

A. The Rose's Roots

It may seem as if the rose goes back to the first day of creation, but in fact the rose is a late bloomer. The species* first appeared less than thirty-five million years ago and took time to diversify. Wild roses* are native to the entire northern hemisphere, but it is in Europe and the Near East that the love affair with roses began. The plants of antiquity and the Middle Ages are known to us, but through imprecise records. It is only beginning with the universal language of botany* in the eighteenth century that reliable information is available concerning hybridization* and extinction.

However, a few varieties of rose that have been so popular that their cultivation can be traced through history. Used from ancient times to decorate soldiers' apparel and chariots, roses spread as a direct result of combat and colonization. The Romans' rose, for example, the white *Rosa* x *alba,* most probably came from their conquest of the East. In twelfth-century Europe, the Crusaders brought the Damask rose* back from the Middle East. Roses from India, China,* and Japan made their way to Europe as a result of mercantile expansion. The complete range of old roses* present in the West by the end of the nineteenth century gave rise to genetic experimentation which led in turn to modern roses.*

B. The Ever-Evolving Rose

Botanical definitions of roses were improved upon by horticultural classifications* based on appearance, growth and development, flowering, and shape—in short, the same characteristics one needs to know to make a perfect bouquet!* Rose categories are not definitive,

Elisabeth-Louise Vigée Le Brun, *Marie-Christine de Bourbon.* Museo e Gallerie Nazionali di Capodimonte, Naples.

David Austin's "Heritage" English rose, 1984.

André Ève's "Prestige de Bellegarde" (*Rosa polyantha*), 1974.

however, mainly because all varieties are in a perpetual state of evolution. The Floribunda* and Polyantha* rose categories were far more distinct twenty years ago, but the edges have blurred due to constant cross-breeding and hybridization. Even the fundamental differences between old and modern roses have been called into question. The standard image of the old rose* is a big cabbage-like flower with a heady fragrance that blooms only once a year, until its volume causes it positively to droop on its weak stem. In turn, modern roses* are seen as producing elongated buds and lacking scent. But some modern roses have been bred to resemble old roses, making it truly difficult to tell them apart. There is really no good reason to take up sides for the new against the old, or vice versa. There is room for both traditional and modern varieties in today's gardens. And who knows what tomorrow's will hold?

C. Breeding Roses

The temptation to experiment with creating new roses has always been hard for gardeners to resist. Nowadays, most rose breeding is done in laboratories by experts, professionals in their own right. The rose industry involves patenting,* marketing, and other commercial activities. The competition is stiff, and only the top outfits reach the international level. But there is nothing to stop talented small-scale professionals and even amateurs from proving their worth at flower shows.* One prize-winning rose can lead to a whole successful career. Like everything else, a rose's long-term popularity is a matter of public opinion, quality, and even the name* it is given.

Creating a new rose entails a great deal of time, money, and hard work. Once the result has met with the highest standards of approval, the new rose is protected by patent laws. Research is the first step in making a new variety. Breeders examine roses in the wild* and in gardens,* combing the world to discover characteristics of interest.

Mathias Tantau's "Cerise Bouquet" shrub rose, 1937.

Preceding double page: Hybrid tea rose.

Miniature rose.

Then a full genetic chart is drawn up in order to determine the strains' inherent strengths and weaknesses. The next stages of their work, crossbreeding and sowing,* can take years and require a whole team working together. These are followed by costly market research and advertising. The days when a truly dedicated amateur such as the Reverend Joseph Pemberton could devote his life to creating ten great new roses are gone. Multinational giants of the rose industry are now firmly established. And a true breakthrough in the field, such as David Austin's development of English roses* in the early 1960s, is a great event.

II. Growing Roses

A. Ornamental . . . and More

One of the reasons for the rose's lasting popularity is its variety of uses in different cultures and at different times. Of its rich symbolic and practical past, the rose today primarily retains its aesthetic value. Some traces of ritual and tradition are still attached to the lovely blooms, however, particularly in its identification with love.

The extent of the use of the rose as a beauty product or adornment, and its association with beauty in ancient times is not really known. One of Homer's most famous epithets refers to "rosy-fingered dawn." But aside from this repeated mention, beauty and roses are not equated in classical texts. More is made of the social importance of the rose as a symbol of wealth and prosperity. In ancient Rome,* laws were enacted to regulate the use of roses. These favorite flowers were also a requisite part of many religious ceremonies.

Nor is it known when perfume* was first invented. The Damask rose came to be prized for its strong fragrance,* and its perfume was

widely used in cosmetics, foodstuffs, and medicines.* The rose's health-giving virtues are still exploited today in the fields of aromatherapy and beauty care.

Decorative wall tiling, Vakil Mosque, Shiraz, Iran.

Roses continue to be intensively cultivated for the production of fragrance. It takes acres worth of rose petals to produce a small quantity of the essential ingredient, attar* or rose oil. Roses also represent the lion's share of florists' profits everywhere. Roses sold by florists are grown in greenhouses and shipped pre-cut. Even minimal improvements in stem quality or indoor staying power are the fruit of costly and lengthy scientific research.

B. Seeds and Stock

Woman Perfuming Herself, c. 1860. Engraving, Bibliothèques des Arts décoratifs, Paris.

Chance plays a major role in evolution and in all forms of innovation. The rose illustrates this beautifully, with its abundant cross-breeding, both spontaneous and controlled. Sometimes a mutation* will give rise to a new variety that is more hardy or propagates more readily from cuttings* or layering. Flower fullness is probably a negative characteristics on a purely biological level, because it hides the reproductive parts from pollen-carrying insects. Therefore, without human intervention, roses would never have became so expansive and ornamental. The early horticulturists worked by sifting through the existing species* of roses to find qualities of interest, planted the best specimens in close proximity, and left the rest up to the birds and bees. Then the new seeds had to be sown* and sorted. This method prevailed up until the early twentieth century, when principles derived from the Austrian monk Gregor Mendel's observations of the lowly pea ushered in the age of genetic* experimentation. Organized attempts to deliberately mix recessive and dominant characteristics followed. Today the search for the blue rose* is at the forefront of advanced genetics.

C. Gardening Know-How

Growing roses means different things in the different contexts of private, professional, and botanical gardens. The rosebush itself comes in a wide variety of shapes, sizes, formats, and containers. Thriving roses can be grown from cuttings, but this practice is left to the amateur gardener, since the hit-or-miss results, and the time and materials required, are not economically feasible for professional nurseries. Growing roses from seeds is an effective method only with species* and wild varieties. Grafting* is the preferred method of rose propagation. In this process, a cultivar (short for "cultivated variety") rose stem is grafted onto a hardy species rose sapling. After two years a successful rose produced in this way is marketed, often as a bareroot rose to be planted during the non-growing season. Along with attentive, ongoing care,* proper planting* in correctly prepared soil makes for a durable rosebush that will provide decades or even a century's worth of gorgeous flowers.

The florist industry has developed stringent requirements for the selection of rootstock (the bush to receive the graft) and intensive forcing* techniques for the production of commercial cut roses. Under these conditions, the plants perform at a high output rate for a few years, and get burned out so quickly they must be replaced.*

Facing page: A harmonious bouquet of garden roses.

III. Philosophy and the Garden

A. Gardens of Eden

Whether in real or imaginary gardens, the rose has always served as a symbol for thinkers and writers. The biblical Garden of Eden was a model for medieval* Christian and Islamic gardens, where an ideal world is enclosed and shielded from harsh reality. Psychologists have likened this protected, walled universe to the womb. Different cultures have associated the roses in such gardens with life's brevity and the pursuit of perfection, as well as quests for earthly, spiritual, or ideal beauty.*

B. A Passion for Collection and Creation

Rose collectors are driven by an admiration for beauty and a thirst for knowledge. Enthusiasm for roses has led to world-wide expeditions, scientific dedication, and creative expression in painting,* poetry* and all the arts. One of the first and most famous comprehensive rose collections was that of the Empress Josephine* at Malmaison, near Paris. Josephine began developing her garden* around the beginning of the nineteenth century, and was soon emulated by other passionate rose collectors, cultivators, and creators. Though the Malmaison gardens are no longer intact, the concept behind them gave rise to the botanical rose garden* as we know it today. Visiting exemplary gardens can be rewarding and edifying for the potential rose grower as well as for the practiced industry professional. It is a chance to compare qualities and characteristics, techniques and compatibilities.

Lambert of St. Omer, *Liber Floridus*, 1448. Musée Condé, Chantilly, France.

C. The Art of the Rose

The way a rose is represented tells a thousand words about the values of a given culture or era. From Minoan frescoes to Islamic miniatures, from medieval rose windows* to nineteenth-century ceiling ornaments, the image of a rose is always laden with meaning, and sometimes shrouded in secrecy.*

The rose "speaks" in the garden as well. It was once considered a plant apart, to be cultivated only among other roses, but today's landscape specialists have proven that roses and other vegetation can gracefully complement each other. The best gardens offer harmonious compositions of color, texture, and scent that are a pure delight.

IV. More than Just a Flower

A. The Mystique of Roses

Whether it is a question of planting a bush or magnifying a flower into a huge stained-glass window, a rose is never just simply a rose. It has served equally as an emblem of peace and war, purity and carnality, an open declaration of love and a plea for strict discretion. Rose insignias have been adopted over the ages by chivalric orders, esoteric organizations, political parties, and even the British Secret Service during World War II.

The rose is also a sign of complicity. According to Roman mythology, Venus gave the god of silence, Harpocrates,* a rose in return for shrouding her affairs in secrecy. In the art of navigation, the compass rose* helped sailors master the four winds. In all its guises, there is more to the rose's beauty than meets the eye . . .

B. Love in All Its Forms

The rose, like the heart, is a primal symbol of love. From Greek mythology to Persian poetry,* the rose evokes earthly delights and carnal yearnings. The favorite flower of Venus, goddess of love, and her son Eros (whose blood is sometimes said to have stained the white rose red), its petals carpeted Roman festivals and orgies, where revelry was held sacred.

Christianity kept the flower but changed its meaning, so that the rose came to stand for spiritual love and purity. The roots of such a transformation go back at least as far as Plato, who divided love into the sacred and the profane. Just as Roman temples were transformed into churches, the rose under Christianity was reincarnated as a sign of the Virgin Mary, and feminine perfection. According to legend,

Rose garden, Parc de Bagatelle, Paris.

Nicholas Hilliard, *Portrait of Queen Elizabeth I.* Walker Art Gallery, Liverpool.

the original rosary* was actually a strand of roses, and there are many accounts of Christian saints and martyrs which involve roses. The rose speaks for every imaginable sort of love.

C. Life and Death

Lucas Cranach, *Martyrdom of Saint Catherine,* 1506. Right panel, *Saints Dorothy, Agnes and Cunegond.* Gemäldegalerie, Dresden.

The rose is an intimate partner in all the main events of life, from birth to death. Why else has it attracted so much attention in religion, literature, and gardening? From the *Thousand and One Nights* to e. e. cummings, the rose's sweetness always has at least a touch of sorrow, just as its lovely petals only partially conceal its thorns. The fact that it decorates both wedding bouquets and funeral wreaths makes the rose all the more poignant as it opens with the first days of spring. But though individual roses may wither and die, the plant survives to blossom another year, and the rose's beauty is eternal.

Philippe Bonduel

ARTHURIAN LEGEND: The Round Table and the Rose

The origins and accuracy of the Arthurian legend have been obscured by the mists of time, but there can be no doubt as to the story's importance to later generations. At the close of the fifteenth century, for example, King Henry VII of England had a replica made of King Arthur's legendary Round Table. The eighteen foot (6 m) diameter table dominated the great hall of Winchester Castle. A Tudor rose with two rows of five petals, one white, the other red, was painted in the center of the table. It was imagined that the mythical Holy Grail would be placed in this spot. Lines spread outward from it toward the designated places of each of the twelve Knights of the Round Table. The round table rose has been interpreted as the emblem of a sect of sun-worshipping mystics, or an esoteric symbol understood only by initiates, but it is also only one part of the legend. Many tales focus instead on the adventures of Arthur's chivalric men, emphasizing their bravery, devotion, and manners. The king and his knights were presented as the perfect example of courtliness—Henry VII even named his firstborn son Arthur. His choice expressed his belief in the past and future greatness of his kingdom, and his aspirations for his heir. Alas, this Arthur died before his sixteenth birthday, and Henry VIII ascended the throne in his stead. JB

"The Lovers" tarot card.

Rose seller in Djebel Akhdar, Oman.

Attar of Roses

The use of perfume* as a cosmetic adornment began as an accidental by-product of hygienic practices. In ancient Mediterranean and Middle Eastern regions, people regularly rubbed themselves down with oil. This served a variety of purposes, from rejuvenating sun-exposed skin to cleaning it, given the relative scarcity of fresh water. Like many substances, oils tend to go bad quickly in warm climates. As a solution to this problem, pleasant-smelling ingredients were added to the oil to mask any disagreeable odors that might arise. This practice proved fortuitous, since oils make fine preservatives for scents.

The development that most revolutionized this process was perfected by the great Persian

Roses gathered for making attar of roses in Grasse, France.

From petals to perfume.

physician and philosopher Avicenna (980–1037) and has not changed much since. Avicenna's method used the still, an Arab invention. The first rosewater, a distillation of rose essence and water, made its appearance in the 1100s. It was not until two centuries later that alcohol came to be used in the distilling process.

Attar of roses (also called otto of roses, rose oil, or essence of rose) is made from the petals of roses, primarily Damasks* and Gallicas.* In Persian, "attar" means "fragrant oil," deriving from the Arabic for "breathing perfume." Attar of roses is non-greasy, and yellow in color. It is so precious that a few drops in a beautiful container made fitting gifts for queens and princesses. According to legend, attar of roses was first created by mistake during the Mongol wedding celebration of Princess Nour-Djihan with the Emperor Djihanguyr. A canal was dug around the garden of the palace and filled with rosewater. As they floated along in a royal bark, the bride and groom noticed the heat of the sun producing a film of rose oil on the surface of the water. It was skimmed off and found to be an exquisite perfume.

Official credit for first separating rose water and attar of roses goes to the famous Swiss alchemist and physician Theophrastus Paracelsus (1493–1541). An efficient process using steam under low pressure is most commonly used today.

Rose petals destined for making attar of roses must be gathered very early in the day because the essence evaporates in the sun. Petals must be distilled immediately to avoid oxidation. Of course, no two roses smell exactly alike. The Damask varieties produce a headier, more straightforward oil, whereas those derived from Gallica blooms are more honeyed and spicy. It takes two and a half tons of rose petals to make a pound of rose oil. PB

SCHMIZO
DURAN 50
SCHOTT
MAINZ

Beauty

Throughout history, many a lover has envisioned his beloved in floral terms: rosy cheeks, rose-red lips, rose-scented. The rose, too, is the most clichéd of Valentine offerings, whether adorning heart-shaped boxes of chocolates or in the form of a dozen long-stemmed crimson blooms. It has given rise to the greatest possible range of romantic expression, from the most trite ditties (Roses are red/Violets are blue/Sugar is sweet/And so are you) to sublime Elizabethan sonnets. The fleeting nature of youth's rosy beauty is readily apparent in Shakespeare's Sonnet 54:

O, how much more doth beauty beauteous seem
By that sweet ornament which truth doth give!
The rose looks fair, but fairer we it deem
For that sweet odour which doth in it live.
The canker-blooms have full as deep a dye
As the perfumed tincture of the roses,
Hang on such thorns and play as wantonly
When summer's breath their masked buds discloses:
But, for their virtue only is their show,
They live unwoo'd and unrespected fade,
Die to themselves. Sweet roses do not so;
Of their sweet deaths are sweetest odours made:
And so of you, beauteous and lovely youth,
When that shall fade, my verse distills your truth.

William Blake also deftly uses the rose's associations with beauty and pure love to create an image of taint in his "Sick Rose":

O Rose, thou art sick!
The invisible worm
That flies in the night,
In the howling storm,

Has found out thy bed
Of crimson joy:
And his dark secret love
Does thy life destroy.

With both roses and people, the fear is that beauty, for all its irresistible appeal, may be only skin deep, that beneath silky, flawless surface lies decay and death.

Edward Burne-Jones, *The King's Daughter.* Musée d'Orsay, Paris.

BLUE

To be human is to dream the impossible dream. After achieving a perfect yellow rose, it is only natural to set out in search of the blue rose. In the 1960s the first near successes yielded odd petals more lilac than truly blue. The "Charles de Gaulle," which first appeared in 1974, is one of the finest examples of these roses. The plants are not hardy and the flowers are rather fragile to the touch, but the scent is full-bodied and heavenly.

But in terms of a real blue, the blue of blueberries or the sky, there is nothing to be found in the rose family's genetic makeup. Thus, barring some astounding genetic mutation,* a naturally blue rose is simply out of the question.

However, the Australian agricultural engineering company Florigene (Calgene Pacific) recently announced the projected release of roses containing a "blue gene" to be marketed at a price of ten dollars each. A flower's color comes from its ability to biosynthesize specific pigments. Roses lack the main enzyme needed for synthesizing the blue pigment delphinidin. Scientists at Florigene have therefore worked toward isolating the "blue gene" from naturally blue flowers and introducing it in roses to promote the biosynthesis of blue pigment. Up until now the pigment's presence is only detectable under laboratory analysis. The work goes on, but success seems within sight. PB

Meilland's "Charles de Gaulle," 1974.

BOTANICAL DEFINITION

Like hawthorn, fruit trees such as apple, cherry and almond trees, and berries such as raspberries, blackberries and strawberries, roses are members of the *Rosaceae* family. Both berries and roses belong to the *Rosoideae* subfamily. They are further distinguished from their close cousins within *Rosoideae* by comprising the genus *Rosa*. Examples of species* within *Rosa* are *pimpinellifolia* or *foetida*, *canina*, *carolina*, and *cassiorhodon*. A distinct plant is ordinarily designated by its genus name (indicated by the term Rosa or its abbreviation R.) written in italics, followed by the species name in lowercase italics to avoid any confusion. Botanists also add to this the name of the person who first described the species according to the official rules of botany. This designation remains set in stone, unless, of course, new findings show it was mistaken. Complications sometimes arise when the species divides into a sub-species on its own, coming up with forms and variants which apply to a portion of the species population in a way that is consistent but not genetically significant enough to call for a new species to be named. Stable variants include color and the absence or presence of fragrance.* Distinctions are often, although not always, noted with abbreviations: SSP stands for sub-species; f. for *forma*; and var. for *varietas* or variation. The term variety officially refers only to spontaneous, individual variants found in the wild.

All horticultural creations are officially known as cultivars, a term derived from the phrase "cultivated variety." Cultivars originate, and remain, in cultivation. In the past, some horticultural experts were in the habit of giving their cultivars Latinate names to make them sound more legitimate. But this is no longer the case with new cultivars today. Horticultural roses are nearly all hybrids* or sprung from mutations.* Natural, spontaneous hybrids are indicated by an x in front of the species name, as in *Rosa* x *hibernica*, a hybrid of *R. pimpinellifolia* and *R. canina*, or in front of the genre name, as in x *Hulthemosa hardii*, a hybrid of *Rosa* and *Hulthemia*. The origin of certain roses is lost to history, and their genealogies are often unclear. In the past this often made scientific identification a challenging and sometimes nerve-wracking process. Today, botanists are aided in their work by advanced laboratory techniques and genetic* analysis. PB

Bourbon

The hybrid* Bourbon rose is a natural crossbreed of Damask and China roses. It emerged on Bourbon, the island known today as Réunion, and was discovered by Edouard Perichon early in the nineteenth century. In 1819, the French botanist Jean-Nicolas Bréon sent some of the seeds to his friend Antonin Jacques, later the gardener of King Louis-Philippe. These yielded the first Bourbon rosebushes which came to play a major role in the development of modern roses.* Bourbon roses have the pronounced fragrance* characteristic of old-fashioned roses.* The bushes are repeat-flowering shrubs. PB

John Waters, *Horticultural roses.* Bibliothèque Nationale de France, Paris.

■ BOUQUET

The rose's natural place is outdoors, as a fragrant bush, a rambling border, or climbing its way up a wall. But the urge to bring beautiful flowers inside, to be admired in a creative bouquet, or alone in an elegant vase, is hard to resist. Once the flowers are cut, the possibilities for arranging them are as limitless as your imagination.

Roses are at the heart of many a florist's art. The roses used commercially come primarily from professional greenhouses, and are priced according to their stem length, thorn size, life-span after cutting, ability to withstand transportation and conservation, and of course their color, shape, and fragrance.* Over the past fifty years, the quality of roses used by florists has greatly improved. Such international growers as Meilland, Kriloff, Kords, and Tantau have contributed to a veritable revolution in the production and quality of commerical roses. Highly fragrant roses which were formerly unavailable in greenhouse production are now increasingly to be found.

Those who have the option of using home grown flowers for bouquets usually make an effort to lay out the garden in such a way that when roses and other flowers are regularly cut they do not leave awkward gaps. It is best to plant rows spaced about two feet (50-60 cm) apart, and group them by variety. It is a good idea to choose hardy bushes with strong stems and long-lasting double flowers. It is also nice to plant some varieties that produce decorative rose hips after the growing season, because these make lovely additions to fall and winter arrangements. Rose species* that generate profuse vegetation, planted separately in hedges or bushes, are highly recommended. Flowers are best cut early in the morning, and preferably right when the buds are beginning to open. The cut blooms should be kept in a cool place and in water until ready to be used for the bouquet. AE

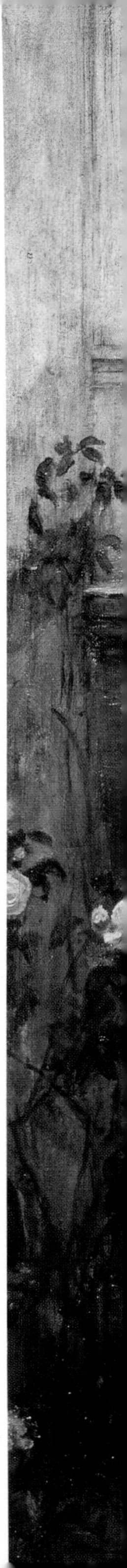

John William Waterhouse, *The Shrine*, 1895.
Christopher Wood Gallery, London.

■ CARE

After planting,* rosebushes still require regular, year round care. In spring and summer, watering is necessary when there is not enough rain, especially when temperatures are high. Roses do not need to be watered as often as some flowers, but the watering should still be abundant and from below. Avoid getting water on the leaves since this can lead to mildew, which is the source of most diseases* in roses. Instead, water the soil around the plants, ideally using a drip irrigation system.

Covering the ground around rosebushes with chopped straw, bark chips, or similar organic matter serves to maintain humidity and prevent weeds from growing. Otherwise, regular weeding is required. This should be done manually to avoid the many adverse effects of chemical weed killers. The best way to weed is with a garden tool, because this also loosens the topsoil.

Insecticides can be used on the leaves—sparingly and according to instructions to minimize risking damage to other plants and the environment.

Roses need light and frequent fertilizing to build strength and disease resistance. Use organic fertilizers such as compost, alfalfa, fish emulsion, manure, bone meal, or kelp. The fertilizer should be worked into the soil around the rosebush during the winter. Rosebushes should also be fertilized after the first flowering. This should be followed by pruning.* If chemical fertilizer is used plants should immediately be generously watered. AE

Breaking up the soil.

Hoeing weeds.

Covering to preserve humidity.

China

Roses enjoyed only limited popularity in ancient China. Nonetheless, they were cultivated and bred there for centuries, yielding results that fascinated the Western botanists who came into contact with them. Chinese roses were imported to Europe in the late seventeenth century and introduced into England. Four of these Chinese roses went on to play a decisive role in horticultural* history. All four are thought to be the result of crossbreeding between the species *Rosa chinensis* and *Rosa gigantea.*

Rosa chinensis was first brought to England by Joseph Banks in 1789, where it was dubbed "Old Blush China" or "Parson's Pink China." This rose was found growing four years later in a Mr. Parson's garden, and was propagated by the grower James Colville. The spindly bush had pale pink, soft flowers. On Réunion, an island in the southern Indian Ocean, *Rosa chinensis* gave rise to the Bourbon* rose through natural crossbreeding. Another repeat-flowering *Rosa chinensis* known as "Slater's Crimson China" or "Semperflorens" was brought to England around 1791. The husky bush and its crimson flowers are no longer in existence today. Contrary to legend, this is not the ancestor of the Portland* rose, which predates its introduction.

In 1809 *Rosa* x *odorata,* known as "Hume's Blush" tea-scented China, was brought over from Canton. The repeat-flowering shrub with its large pale pink flowers is fragile and highly susceptible to frost. The blooms give off the hallmark "Chinese tea" scent which was passed on to its hybrids. John Parks presented the *Rosa* x *odorata* known as "Parks' Yellow" tea-scented China rose to the Royal Horticultural Society of England in 1824. The fourth of the historic China roses, it has the pale yellow color highly prized in old* roses.

These "Four Stud Chinas" as the group of roses came to be called, are all repeat-flowering, and have smooth leaves and sparse thorns. They were crossed with Gallica* and Damask* varieties to give rise to a number of repeat-flowering roses. PB

All plants, knowing that spring
will soon be gone,
Their brightest rosebud purple
hues put on:
And from each bloom
Comes sweet perfume.

Han Yü, "Late Spring," Tang Dynasty

Chinese wall paper (detail), c. 1760

Compass Rose

The compass rose has been embellishing charts, maps and compasses since the fourteenth century. The term comes from the figure's rose-like appearance. It was designed to be used for sailing and was originally called a "wind rose" because it shows the directions of the wind. Its thirty-two points comes from the directions of the eight major winds, the eight half-winds, and the sixteen quarter-winds. JB

Luis Lazaro, Compass rose (detail), 1563. Academy of Sciences, Lisbon.

Crown of Roses

In ancient times, the rose was both a symbolic and devotional object, ever present on important occasions. Roses were offered to the gods and used as a talisman or sacred object. Specially blessed blooms were commonly worn as a headpiece or necklace, and were thought to offer protection and to help the wearer commune with divine beings. In the third century, Atheneus wrote that the wearer of the most flowers will be most smiled upon by the gods and that a crown of roses, the sign of divine favor, should be worn during sacrifices. Roman* brides wore crowns of roses, and the Roman festival of roses, *Rosalia*, was celebrated every spring.

In Judaism, the Talmud instructs the groom to don a crown of roses, a custom also prevalent in ancient Persia and India. In Christianity, a crown of white roses came to symbolize feminine virtue, and might be worn by a bride or by a nun when taking her vows of spiritual union with Christ, while saints are also sometimes portrayed wearing a crown of roses. JB

Film still from *Thérèse,* directed by Alain Cavalier, 1986.

CUTTING AND LAYERING

Since they are natural climbers and creepers, many roses tend to grow in layers. When their long branches touch the ground, they root to form a new growth several yards from the original plant. In the wild or an abandoned garden, roses can turn into tangled brambles. On the positive side, this means a rose-lover can simply cover a young branch with earth, sit back, and wait for it to grow. In a year's time, a new plant will appear, and can be easily separated for transplanting elsewhere. In this way, layering is like a natural form of growth from cuttings. In the strict sense of the term, the process of cutting does not occur in nature, but consists of separating promising branches, and planting them in the hope that they will take root. This is often the case, thanks to root-promoting hormones that are activated in branches deprived of nourishment. Timing is important: the cut branch should be fully developed, but not yet hard enough to prevent new roots from coming through. Summer is generally the best time of year for this. A powdered synthetic hormone compound can be sprinkled on the cut end to promote rapid rooting. The ideal branch should measure just under eight inches (20 cm) in length, with all except the topmost leaf removed. It should be placed in a well-lit spot protected from wind and too much sun, halfway covered in the soil. Cuttings should not be moved before the following spring. The advantage of growing rose bushes from cuttings is that it is a simple operation with a high success rate, and generally, barring mutation,* yields a faithful replica of the original. The disadvantage compared to grafting* is that the process is material-intensive, and there is no guarantee that the bush from the cutting will adapt to transplanting elsewhere, a problem not an issue with grafting. PB

A rose branch cutting being planted.

Meilland's "Bingo." A self-layering variety.

Damask Roses

The Damask rose is a spontaneous crossbreed of a Gallica* rose and the species* *Rosa phoenicea.* Damask roses are assumed to have been brought to Europe from the East by the Crusaders.

Damasks have handsome shrubs with light pink, highly fragrant* flowers. Autumn Damasks are less decorative, but hold the distinction of being the first repeat-flowering roses to be grown in Europe, long before the introduction of Chinese* roses in the eighteenth century. Autumn Damasks may have already existed in the west by the first century B.C.E., as Virgil makes mention of a twice-flowering rose in the *Georgics.* PB

"Ispahan," or "Pompon des Princes," Damask rose, 1832.

DISEASE

Despite their reputation, roses are, on the whole, hardy plants capable of living even in less-than-ideal conditions. But in addition to the many insects that like to feast on rose leaves—from ladybugs to leaf-cutter ants to red spiders—their foliage is susceptible to a few debilitating diseases. The main diseases to which roses fall prey are blackspot, powdery mildew, downy mildews, and rose rust. These are all types of fungus and can be effectively treated with fungicides. It is important to apply fungicides at the first signs of disease, or to use them preventively, before the onset of hot and humid weather when these fungi thrive.

Until vaccinations or new genetic strains come along, it will be inevitable for almost all rosebushes to contract blackspot at some point. This disease can be identified by the appearance on the leaves of brown spots ringed in yellow. If blackspot is not stopped immediately, it can go on to overtake the whole bush and neighboring plants. If it strikes, the only way to check it is through severe pruning. Once the affected parts have been removed they should be disposed of far away from the area where plants are growing. Downy mildew covers rose leaves and buds with a white down that quickly kills them. Like powdery down and rose rust, it should be treated in the same way as blackspot.

To prevent disease in rosebushes, use fertilizers specially recommended for roses, and whenever possible water the plants in the morning, at the roots rather than from above. The bushes should be pruned regularly to ensure good air circulation, and dead or weak leaves and stems should be promptly cut away. Sun destroys fungus, and this is one of the many arguments in favor of making sure rosebushes get enough exposure to light.

Infestation by insects can be prevented with the careful and selective use of insecticides. Avoid getting insecticide on the flowers themselves, since this could be harmful to bees and other insects useful for roses. AE

Onset of blackspot disease.

Downy mildew disease.

David Austin's "Constance Spry" English rose, 1961.

English Roses

Ever since the early seventeenth century, when English explorers began bringing the lush vegetation of China* and the Far East back home with them, British botanists have played a decisive role in the development of the rose. When the English East India Company's offices opened in Macao and Canton in 1699, they also ensured the future splendor of English botanical gardens.

The nineteenth century was the golden age of English roses, with such great growers as William Paul, the Dicksons, and Lord Penzance, creator of the *Eglanteria* hybrids,* leading the way. The rosebush's leaves were bred to give off a delicate apple fragrance.* In the early twentieth century the Reverend Joseph Pemberton successfully cross-bred the musk rose (*Rosa moschata)* with remontant (repeat-flowering) varieties.

Next came the development of the modern* rose by the great

David Austin's creeping "Constance Spry" English rose, 1961.

David Austin's "The Pilgrim" English Rose, 1991.

English nurseries of R. and Jack Harkness, Sam McGredy, and—once again—the Dicksons. Today, Peter Beales is one of the top specialists in old-fashioned roses.* In the 1950s, Beales and Graham Thomas contributed to bringing back old-fashioned blooms. This led hybrid specialists to develop modern repeat-flowering roses with the shape and fragrance* of old-fashioned varieties.

In 1961, David Austin achieved the first highly successful crossbreed between the Floribunda* "Dainty Maid" and the Gallica "Belle Isis." This crossing of an early modern tea rose with an old variety was the first of what very soon came to be called English roses. It was christened "Constance Spry," in honor of the leading florist of the time. This large bush or creeping rose has large, double, cup-shaped flowers with a delicate pink hue and the scent of myrrh. The "Constance Spry" is the first in a long line created by Austin, often with the encouragement or collaboration of Graham Thomas. The descendants of the "Constance Spry" have been bred to attain the fullness of peonies, a heady but refined scent, lush, robust foliage, and constant flowering up to autumn. These varieties require rich soil and heavy fertilizing. AE

Floribunda

Along with hybrid tea roses,* Floribunda roses are among the most popular in gardens today. This modern* rosebush is wonderfully hardy, and yields a great abundance of vividly colored blooms. Floribundas are descendants of a cross of hybrid tea roses with *Rosa polyantha.** They are therefore also called Hybrid Polyanthas. The first Floribunda was developed in 1912 by the Poulsens, a Danish family of rose breeders. The Poulsens aimed to create roses that could withstand the Scandinavian climate. Floribunda means "flowering in abundance." This is a fitting name for plants which blossom in generous clusters. It also differentiates them from their hybrid tea parents and typical modern roses, which have one flower per stem.

Floribunda roses are prized for their massed color effects. They

Jack Harkness's "Escapade" Floribunda, 1967.

are often used for hedgerows, borders, foundation covers, and to create mounds of color in the garden. Sometimes they are called "landscape roses." They are hardy and re-bloom more quickly and readily than other varieties. PB

Flower Shows

Like poodles and Persian cats, roses regularly appear in shows which are attentively followed by aficionados, amateur and professional alike. Shows in different regions and countries allow growers to judge how their prize blooms may hold up in different climes.

The roses are marked only by numbers in order to maintain anonymity and impartiality among the judges. Some competitions request the jury to judge the entries over a period of time, and a second jury to judge them on the day of the actual show. Prize categories often include shrub hardiness, shape, fragrance,* and a host of other qualities. But it is innovation that brings top honors, and a gold medal is sure to help sell a rose.

Rose-lovers in Europe and North America can follow the rounds from one show to the next from May through September. High points of the rose show circuit include the Chelsea Flower Show in mid-May in London, the Hampton Court Palace Flower Show and British Rose Festival in mid-July at the Royal Horticultural Society in London, the annual Glasgow Rose Trials, and the annual American Rose Society Conventions. Other important rose shows take place in Le Roeulx in Belgium, Orleans in France, Geneva, Rome, Madrid, The Hague, and Baden-Baden. PB

Climbing rose.

Forcing

Even in antiquity, the very high demand for roses led to attempts to prolong their growing season. An early method for forcing growth involved digging a ditch around the plant and filling it with warm water when the first buds appeared. The simplest technique, still in use to this day, is to grow roses in a warm climate and to transport them to new locations as quickly and efficiently as possible. An additional method is to control production and growing by creating self-contained greenhouse environments. This approach was employed by the ancient Romans,* who developed shelters with removable lids. These shed-like structures were irrigated by canals that brought in warm water from thermal springs and were covered at night.

Forcing as we know it today began with the invention of the modern greenhouse. The

first were complete with windows, but still initially relied on thermal spring water for heating. Successful growing was largely a mater of genetics.* Roses often did best when grafted* to *Rosa indica* "Major" rootstocks, which flourish in warmer climates and are capable of sharing this predilection with their grafts. Grafts were also chosen from cultivars that grow best indoors.

For practical reasons today's plants are usually maintained out of the ground, in neutral substrates that are watered and fertilized with scientific precision. Today's greenhouses are heated, ventilated, shaded, and electronically monitored to produced flowers year-round. This is the method used to produce roses sold through florists. At home, you can get a head start on outdoor blooming by partially forcing rosebushes in heated greenhouses. Buds should appear by late April or early May. PB

Meilland's "Starlite" roses growing in a greenhouse.

Portrait of Sultan Mehmet II,
c. 1475.
Topkapi Palace, Istanbul.

Fragrance

There is nothing more subjective than the sense of smell, and the scent of each rose is different. It is made up not only of the flowers, but of the stem, leaves, and all the plant's parts in combination. The smell of roses from a particular bush also depends on the conditions under which the plant was grown. A shrub raised in full sunlight will create different odors than one grown in a dark, damp climate.

Fragrance is an important consideration in the experimentation of rose breeders. They study the chemicals present in different parts of plants, especially those concentrated in the petals, and how these chemicals interact with each other and the environment. Factors contributing to fragrance include resins, pH levels, and fatty acids.

Rosa centifolia has the scent of carnations. *Rosa rubiginosa* and *Rosa macrantha* give off a

woodsy apple smell. *Rosa lutea* wafts lemony notes. The leaves of *Rosa muscosa* exude a special hint of camphor. Not all rose odors are entirely agreeable, however. *Rosa foetida*, for example, smells faintly of stinkbug!
Legend would have it that tea roses* owe their fragrance to the exotic teas with which they were imported. But it is really the roses themselves which produce these perfumes by turns reminiscent of violets, lemon, licorice, grapefruit, and even banana and vanilla.
A rose's fragrance also changes with temperature and time of day, and of course depends upon the mood of whomever is smelling the bloom. With all the delicious subtleties and variables involved, the best approach is simply to explore the scents of roses oneself. PB

Rosa gallica "Versicolor."

Gallica

The Gallica or Apothecary rose is also known as the Rose of Provins, after a French town near Paris where they are especially plentiful, and which has a long history of perfume* production. The Gallica's native environment is central and southern Europe, extending eastward to Turkey. Its bushes usually grow to about three to four feet (1 m). Their elegant, prickly branches spread out in natural abundance. This species* typically has pink flowers with round red hips in the fall.
Gallicas were grown by the ancient Greeks and Romans.* They are the oldest of all old* roses, and the most hybrid.* As early as the late sixteenth century, there was a semi-double variety whose petals had

Rosa gallica complicata.

variegated pink-white tones. This is the ever-popular "Versicolor" rose. In 1629, the English botanist John Parkinson recorded twelve variations of Gallica roses. These were so intensively hybridized by Dutch, and later French, horticulturists that there were more than a thousand different Gallica types by 1800. Many of them no longer exist, but others are still going strong.

Gallica rosebushes blossom abundantly, and they are generally highly fragrant. Their silky flowers tend to take on fascinating gray, mauve, and even blue nuances before fading. PB

Gardens to Visit

There is no more pleasant and rewarding way to become acquainted with roses than to stroll among them in a garden in the month of June, gaining first-hand knowledge of the effects produced by different rose varieties and planting styles. There are many outstanding rose gardens throughout the United States. The Morcom Amphitheater of Roses in Oakland, California, has over five hundred rose species,* and a special collection of historic hybrid tea roses from the first half of the twentieth century. The large New York Botanical

Garden contains the Peggy Rockefeller Rose Garden, with an extensive selection of modern* and old roses.* England also overflows with wonderful rose gardens open to the public. At the garden of the National Rose Society in Saint Albans, there are over thirty thousand roses to be seen and smelled. They are imaginatively displayed, and the staff is knowledgeable. In the south of England, the Mottisfont Abbey Garden in Hampshire has an exceptional collection of over three hundred varieties of old roses in a wonderful old walled setting. A breathtaking garden, considered by some the height of perfection, is at Sissinghurst Castle in Kent. It was created by the writer Vita Sackville-West, who once claimed to be "drunk on roses." If you are visiting Paris at some time between late May and October, the roses in the Parc de Bagatelle are a sight for sore eyes. The Roseraie du Val-de-Marne, France's national rose conservatory, is located in the suburbs of Paris, and holds more than 3,500 old varieties. There are many other spectacular rose gardens to visit in Europe and throughout the world. PB

Rose garden at the Parc de Bagatelle, Paris.

GATHER YE ROSEBUDS WHILE YE MAY

Ring a ring of roses
A pocket full of posies
Ashes, ashes
We all fall down

The words to this ever-popular nursery game are no childish rhyme, but in fact a subject of heated debate. Some folklorists date the verse back to the Black Death, a mid-fourteenth-century plague. Others trace it to the London plague of 1665. Some defenders of the plague theories hold that the first line refers to the round red rashes which were an early symptom of plague. The second line is sometimes thought to refer to an alleged method of warding off the disease: stuffing your pockets full of posies. According to others, the virus of the plague had both human and rose hosts in its life cycle. Medieval botanists apparently noticed that the sign of the infestation in the rose was a colored ring around the stem of the rose, which accounts for the first line. Posies, steeped in an herbal tea, were a folk remedy for the infestation, which explains the second line. The final two lines support obvious interpretations of sickness and dying.

While some protest that the rhyme may date only as far back as the nineteenth century and has nothing to do with illness, the words do seem to reflect, however accidentally, the brevity of youth, if not life itself.

With its delicate freshness and ephemeral beauty, the rose has long served as an reminder of the fleetingness of youth and the fragility of life. One of the most popular expressions of this theme is found in Robert Herrick's seventeenth-century poem "To the Virgins, to Make Much of Time":

Edward Burne-Jones, *Pilgrim at the Gate of Idleness* (detail), 1874. Bridgeman Art Library, London.

Gather ye rosebuds while ye may,
Old time is still a-flying;
And this same flower that smiles today
Tomorrow will be dying.

The glorious lamp of heaven, the sun,
The higher he's a-getting,
The sooner will his race be run,
And nearer he's to setting.

That age is best which is the first,
When youth and blood are warmer;
But being spent, the worse, and worst
Times will succeed the former.

Then be not coy, but use your time,
And, while ye may, go marry;
For, having lost but once your prime,
You may forever tarry.

GENETICS
Making Luck Work

The rose's genetic portrait has yet to be painted in full detail. The genetic characteristics of roses, especially when it comes to hybrids,* are highly diverse and complex, and not always apparent, even to the trained analyst.
Like all living things, the cells in roses are diploid (composed of chromosome pairs), except for the reproductive cells which are haploid (composed of a single chromosome chain).
Male and female haploid cells come together to create diploid cells capable of becoming a plant. The offspring will be identical to its parents in cases of self-fertilization or crossed fertilization of sibling rosebushes. But a unique result will spring from

parent plants of different species* or cultivars. Genetic makeup can change due to mutation,* and this too affects offspring.
As Gregor Mendel demonstrated long ago with his peas, not all genes are equal nor outcomes predictable. For example, when a yellow creeping rose is crossed with a red bush rose, one might expect an orange shrub rose. In reality though, it is only safe to say that the result will likely be a climbing red rose. Creeping is a dominant characteristic. So is the male parent's color. Color in the female parent and bushiness in the male parent are recessive characteristics.
Recessive characteristics never disappear, they merely go dormant and reappear through breeding, and it is a challenge for rose breeders to bring them out. Science can be used to second-guess outcomes and inform procedures, but it has not yet reached the point of infallibly determining the results. PB

Everything you need to make a hybrid.

GRAFTING YOUR OWN ROSES

Despite attempts at in vitro rose production, grafting remains the tried and true way to invent new rose variations. Nearly all of the commercial roses available today come from grafting. Grafting has the advantages of being surefire, fast, and low-cost. It can be carried out by first-time amateurs as well as professional horticulturists.

An important first step in grafting is the choice of rootstock on which your bud stick or "scion" is to grow. The climate in your area and the soil type in your garden are the next most important factors. As a rule of thumb, *Rosa multiflora* is a good bet for root stock. If you want to create standard or tree roses, try *Rosa rugosa* or *Rosa canina.*

Cut back the branches and growth of the rootstock to nearly ground level. Then choose and clip bud sticks from young but fully mature branches of the rose to be grafted. The bud sticks should be three to four inches (8 to 10 cm) long, with the leaves removed. Wrap the bud sticks in a damp rag until ready to be used.

The only real tool you need is a razor-sharp knife. There are special grafting knives available, but really any sharp knife will do. Cuts should be made as evenly and straight as possible.

An easy first-time method is to cut a thin strip of bark from a rootstock stem that is slightly thicker than a standard pencil. Next, remove a similar strip from the bud stick, and align the two cuts. Wrap the two tightly together with half-inch (1.25 cm) wide budding tape.

If winters are very cold in your area, you may want to do this in autumn and leave the tape in place until the spring. For summer grafting, the tape can be removed after four to six weeks.

You can try a few grafts with the same rootstock. If the experiment is a success, you should have a new rose by spring. PB

Cutting the bud stem.

A cut bud stem.

Aligning the bud stem and rootstock.

Ernest Quost, *Roses,* 1909. Musée d'Orsay, Paris.

Harmony in the Garden

Boccaccio describes the perfect "garden of abundance" in the *Decameron:* "As for the edges of the paths, they were entirely hidden by the white and vermilion rosebushes. In the morning, and even toward midday, one could roam everywhere with delight in their fragrant shade, without ever being touched by the sun's rays." It seems fitting that roses should predominate in the ideal garden. But the most beautiful arrangements of roses in gardens today are paradoxically not to be found in world-famous rose gardens.* These are scientific spaces, planned to provide the expert rose lover with grounds for comparison and study. Rather, it is often in more modest gardens that perfection may be found.

Even in a garden strictly dedicated to roses, the addition of bright perennials, herbs, or even vegetables provides a sense of novelty and variation in terms of contrast and volume. A few blue blooms offset the absence of that hue in rose varieties. Plants with silver-toned leaves similarly provide contrast with the roses' foliage. The wide variety of roses to choose from makes rose gardening a rewarding and creative task. It would perhaps be a shame to stick to only one type of rose, and refreshing alternatives can be found by combining diverse climbing, bush, shrub, standard, wild,* old,* and modern* roses in just the right quantities and colors. Another fulfilling challenge is to create a garden with flowers that come into bloom at different times, from spring to mid-autumn, thus keeping the roses out of flower from seeming like holes in the fabric.

With a rose garden everything is possible, as far as your imagination, effort, and skill will take you. A good way to make it all seem more manageable is to make a point of regularly visiting smaller rose gardens, both public and private, and making sure to take good notes there for later use. Finally, a green thumb helps, of course, and so does a good eye. PB

■ HORTICULTURAL CLASSIFICATION

While it may be relatively easy to identify wild roses or species* of cultivated blooms, things get tricky when it comes to horticultural hybrids. Like tulips, roses are classified more according to practicalities (based on appearance and optimal growing conditions) than according to scientific considerations. Because stock varies from year to year, the system is designed to adapt to new varieties as well as the changes in the popularity or characteristics of existing varieties.

To understand what the growers' catalogues are referring to, it is necessary know the different categories. Roses are first of all classed according to bush morphology:

- Dwarf or bush roses run from just under two feet to three and a half feet (0.6 to 1.2 m) in size.
- Shrub roses can grow up to ten feet (3 m) before having trouble supporting the weight of their branches and blooms.
- Climbing roses are technically comprised of vines. Their long, flexible branches can reach from nine feet to fifteen yards (3 to 15 m), and as much as sixty yards (60 m) in some cases, such as *Rosa banksiae* "Lutea." For the sake of convenience, bush roses with long branches are added to these category. These include "sports" or genetic mutations of bush varieties. The abbreviation *clb.* is often used to designate climbing roses, whether they be vines, branching bushes, or cultivars. Non-vine climbers are generally stiffer than the vine types.
- Groundcover roses are also vine-like. They are divided into two groups: rambling groundcover roses which grow directly along the ground, and soft, full bushes that often expand through natural layering. The recently developed "landscape" roses, capable of covering extended open space, come under this category.
- Miniature roses are diminutive versions of shrub roses. They are primarily of recent origin and yield perfectly scaled-down flowers on bushes less than a foot (30 cm) tall. Growers specializing in miniature roses offer several hundred varieties, with nearly every kind of rose available in reduced size.
- Standard, or tree roses, grow out from pedicel tips. They are classic roses grafted to bloom on a *Brier*, *Rugosa* or other strong stem. Rosebushes thus become long-stem support systems, and the vine-like types curve and droop (or are trained to do so), like weeping willows.

Within the above categories, roses are further classified in terms of whether they are remontant (repeat-flowering) or bloom once a year. Remontant roses bloom once in the summer and a second time in the fall. Single-flowering varieties bloom only once, but often in dazzling abundance. PB

Standard
or tree rose.

Shrub rose.

Hybridizing

Methods for creating new roses have not changed that much over time. Making a hybrid starts with choosing the "parent" roses to cross-pollinate. These are the plants that will carry and nourish the seeds to maturity. Once the plants have been selected, the "mother" rose must be stripped of its petals by pulling them off right when they are ready to open from bud—although it is hard to keep this step from sounding at least slightly cruel. The stripped pistil should be covered with a wax paper bag or a similar container to keep passing insects from pollinating them. Two days later, pollen from the "father," which has been gathered in a mature, powdery state, is spread on the pistil with a brush, a pipe cleaner, or a finger, and once again covered with the protective bag.

To ensure at least some level of success, the same procedure should be repeated a dozen times with different pistils and pollen from the same two parents. It is a good idea to work in the still calm air of early morning. The process is not difficult but demands concentration, precision, and patience, as well as a healthy dose of good luck. Attach a label to the neck of the bloom noting the name of the mother rose first, followed by the name of the pollen source father. Or use the color-coded string and notebook entry method.

If it doesn't rain too much during the following week or so, if the plants are not attacked by insects or disease, and should the parent plants turn out to be genetically compatible, rose hips will form in the fall, containing the precious hybridized seeds. These are then ready for harvesting and sowing.* PB

Josephine, the Empress of Roses

In 1799, Napoleon Bonaparte's first wife, Josephine, purchased Malmaison, a grand country house near Versailles. By 1814, Josephine had been Empress of France for ten years, and her garden contained every species of rose then known. After her 1809 divorce, Josephine retained her rank and title, and was granted full sovereignty over her Malmasion property, and by 1829 there were 2,562 different roses in her garden.

Europe was re-awakened to the possibilities of ornamental rose gardening by the Empress' enthusiasm for the blooms. Josephine, one of whose middle names was Rose, may have originally become such an assiduous gardener to help pass the time while her husband was occupied with campaigns and

Three steps to pollinating a rose.

politics. She surrounded herself with the great botanists of Europe. Her patronage and passion led directly to the first controlled cross-breeding practices in the West—and to the development of many new varieties of roses. At a time when most European roses bloomed only once a year, many of the roses in Josephine's collection were repeat-blooming or remontant.

Josephine spared no expense when it came to acquiring a coveted plant. Her favorite rose supplier was an English merchant called John Kennedy. Even in the midst of bloody war, the Empress made sure that Kennedy was granted a special passport. And even when France was subject to an otherwise complete maritime blockade, Kennedy was permitted safe passage to deliver new and rare roses. One of the most prized roses imported for the Malmaison garden was the *Rosa indica fragrans.*

The Belgian artist Pierre-Joseph Redouté, who had been a court painter to Marie Antoinette, had a great gift for painting flowers, and was employed by Josephine at Malmaison. Redouté's paintings of the garden there provide contemporary gardeners with an invaluable visual record of roses growing two hundred years ago.

The most dedicated of the horticulturists developing new cultivars for Josephine's garden was Jacques-Louis Descemet, who kept meticulous notes on his cross-breeding activities. Later, with Napoleon exiled, Josephine dead, the nursery sacked by invading English troops, and Malmaison in ruins, Jean-Pierre Vibert, a former soldier in Napoleon's army, bought what was left of Descemet's nursery and notebooks, and managed to salvage a portion of the progress that had been made. PB

Jean Louis Victor Vigier du Vigneau, *The Rose of Malmaison,* 1866. Château de Malmaison, France.

■ LOCATION

Roses like sunlight. They usually do best and flower most in full sun. But some roses look most beautiful planted in the shade, along walls that face east or west and get sun only part of the day.

This habitat is ideal for certain yellow or violet-tinted roses, which are overpowered by too much direct light.

Roses should be planted far from big trees that will deprive them of light. Smaller trees and high hedges are also to be avoided, since partial shadow will lead to an uneven, spotty development of the rosebush. Climbing roses yield more blooms on a well-lit wall, trellis, or arbor. Rose catalogues now offer varieties* suited for northern exposure, but in fact the plants, seeking light and heat, rapidly become very sparse at the

bottom and flower only high up. Rosebushes should be planted in thick, deep soil that has been fertilized with organic matter. A crucial factor is the stock plant's adaptability to the chosen terrain. Only *Rosa canina* stock, for example, can hold up in chalky soil without developing disease. This hardy stock is virtually all-purpose and should be used by anyone looking for easy success with roses. Rosebushes naturally prefer to be planted in the earth, but they can easily adapt to large planters, pots, and terrace gardens if the soil is at least twenty inches (50 cm) deep. Good drainage is also essential; so is regular watering and fertilizing. The best roses to use for potting are repeat-flowering species with small or medium-sized flower clusters. AE

LOVE
A Language of Colors

Roses have long been used to speak of love. In the language of roses, color conveys the lover's intentions. A white rose speaks of purity, virginity, innocence, courtly love, and spiritual adoration. The red rose proclaims passion and suffering in the name of love.

In ancient mythology, the first rose was white,* a reminder of the Golden Age as a time of virtue and innocence. According to Western myths, the red rose was born of the blood spilled when the gods made violent love to mortals. An Eastern tradition suggests that the red rose comes from a smile breathed in the ecstasy of lovemaking.

Christianity frowned upon such associations of the rose with the pleasures of the flesh. The language of the rose was used to express religious devotion and faith, emphasizing spiritual rather than physical love. Church traditions attached new meaning to roses and rose bushes: the red rose was seen to signify Christ's blood, and the white rose became a symbol of the Virgin Mary and, by extension, of piety and sanctity. Crowns of roses* have been worn by brides and by nuns taking their vows, and also by saints.

With the Renaissance came a resurgence of the rose's pagan meanings. Even the Victorians used the language of flowers, particularly roses, to express affection. Today, the red rose still says "I love you." JB

Lorenzo Veneziano, *Virgin and Child,* 1372. Musée de Louvre, Paris.

The Making of a Rose

Creating a whole new rose is a great temptation. Amateur rose lovers have two methods available to them. The first way is to spot a promising mutation and try to propagate it by grafting.* This is the easier, though less common, route. The second approach is to engineer a hybrid.* This entails finding two compatible plants, one female and one male, which have the same number of chromosomes and have characteristics that could make an interesting match in terms of color, scent, abundance of flowers, hardiness, resistance to disease,* etc. It is then a matter of hoping that these characteristics come out in the offspring, and that the weaknesses don't take precedence over the strengths. If a climbing rose is crossed with a yellow one, it is in hope of making a yellow climber. But outcome doesn't always follow intention. Fortunately, there are some rules of thumb to go by. For example,

"Kiftsgate" climbing rose (*Rosa filipes*), 1938.

the female plant is dominant in terms of shrub appearance, whereas the male side is dominant for color.

Professionals make use of technology and the latest botanical research. They painstakingly document and chart the genealogical characteristics of roses and the outcomes of crossbreeding. They also have at their disposal the patience and know-how to bring out a recessive characteristic through multiple crossbreeding for new generations.

However, beginner's luck has been known to play an important role, and many fine old-fashioned roses* are the result of intuition. Natural mutation also plays a part. The well-loved cultivar "Kiftsgate," a spontaneous variant of *Rosa filipes,* originated in Kiftsgate Garden near Hidcote, England, in 1938, and went on to spread throughout the entire world. PB

Medicine

The ancient Greeks and Romans* valued roses as much for their medicinal qualities as for their beauty. Hippocrates, Dioscorides, and Pliny are among those who extolled the rose's multiple healing properties, Pliny going so far as to call it a panacea. The twelfth-century German mystic, Hildegarde von Bingen, prescribed the rose to prevent both moodiness and anger. In the eighteenth century, rose poultices were often used to treat heart palpitations, while a mixture of lemon and rosewater cooked with sugar was a treatment to prevent poisoning and to ward off germs.

Rose cures were perhaps most sworn by in Elizabethan England, and the poems of Shakespeare and others are strewn with rose references. The rose's virtues are lauded in the 1597 *Gerard's Herbal,* one of the first major English books on flowers and plants.

Rosa rugosa rose hips.

Discourse on the Virtues of the Rose. Engraving. Symphorien Champier, *Rosa gallica.* Paris, 1514.

The 1629 gardening classic, *Parkinson's Paradisus,* explains that "the Rose is exceeding great use with us; for the Damask Rose (besides the super-excellent sweet water it yeeldeth being distilled, or the perfume of the leaves being dryed, serving to fill sweet bags) serveth to cause solubleness of the body, made into a Syrup, or preserved with Sugar moist or dry candied. The white rose is much used for the cooling of heat in the eyes; divers doe make an excellent yellow color of the juice of white Roses, where some Allome is dissolved, to color flowers or pictures." And Nicholas Culpeper, another esteemed authority, stated in his 1652 *English Physician* that the rose is ruled by Jupiter, Venus, and the moon, and every part of the flower, from roots to hips, has a variety of medical uses. He claims, for example, that "a decoction of red roses made with wine is very good for the headache, pain in the eyes, throat and gums... The husks of the rose with the beards and nails are binding and cooling."

Rose hips are high in vitamin C, and have been used to prevent scurvy among sailors. Today the rose's beneficial qualities are often exploited in the fields of aromatherapy and healthcare products. JB

Pietro de Crescenzi, *The Garden,* c. 1460. Musée Condé, Chantilly, France.

Medieval Gardens

The rose held a place of honor in medieval gardens, one perhaps even greater than it holds today. There were many reasons for this, from roses medicinal,* alimentary, magical* and symbolic properties to their inspirational beauty.

Ever since the garden of Eden, whose description in the Bible is like that of a dazzling oasis in the middle of harsh desert wasteland, Judeo-Christian imagery and imaginations have cherished the idea of the perfect garden where innocence, virtue, and harmony reign. Similarly, the Koran makes mention of a garden where the just will dwell in the next life. This holy book of Islam also sums up the ancient Arabic world's belief in the importance of gardens: "Bread feeds the body, indeed, but flowers feed also the soul." Throughout the Islamic world, roses flourished in modest courtyards and sumptuous palaces alike. In medieval Persia, there were *paridaezas,* refreshing, enclosed, irrigated gardens in which beguiling animals wandered amid the flowers.

Such roses were brought to Europe by returning crusaders. Not only were the flowers introduced to Europe, the idyllic layout of the Muslim garden itself was also transposed. The arrangement included fruit trees, fragrant green myrtle shrubs, the sound and sight of flowing water and bubbling fountains, and, of course, roses. The scheme greatly influenced the structure of monastic gardens, whether constructed in cloisters or in the open, tended by monks or nuns. A verdant cloister, with its foliage and sparse roses leading to a central font, invites introspection and contemplation, religious or otherwise. The central setting of the *Romaunt of the Rose,** one of the great works of medieval literature, is such a garden where the beloved dwells in safety.

Vegetables and herbs were also grown alongside roses in the medieval garden. A reminder of this can be seen in some small household gardens in Europe, where a spindly rose tree is sometimes to be caught drooping over vegetable patches. As now, a good number of medieval garden enthusiasts wrote about the best techniques, methods, and plants to be used. Nearly all the plants in monastery gardens were on the list of medicinal herbs included in Charlemagne's ninth-century *Capitulare de Villis,* which detailed the plants he sought to have grown throughout the realm. A mid-fifteenth century book in the same genre is *The Feate of Gar-*

deninge by Master Ion Gardener. The medieval authorities' proscriptions and prescriptions were more stringent than what we may be accustomed to, and laden with superstitious caveats. These serious warnings may seem impractical to us, but they often contained a measure of common sense. JB

Modern Roses

In the annals of roses, the modern age began in 1867 with the appearance of the first hybrid tea rose,* "La France." For generations to come, the rage for modern roses almost entirely eclipsed interest in old roses,* and it was not until recent decades that the old rose came back into fashion. Even now, the typical image of a rose corresponds to the modern rose's large, saturated petals unfurling from a big teardrop bud on a long, stiff stem. Modern roses are nearly all repeat-flowering. They generally bloom first in the summer and again in the fall.

Rather like the New World, "La France" was discovered accidentally by someone looking to arrive at a different goal, in this case a gardener trying to develop a bright yellow rose with large petals. The first hybrid teas stunned and delighted Victorian flower lovers with their dramatic blooms and prominent buds. The long stems set the flower off and were ideal for cutting and use in bouquets, and the smaller shrubs made growing roses possible for city dwellers with smaller garden plots.

Floribundas,* developed by the Poulsen family in Holland in 1912, came from crossing Polyantha* and hybrid tea roses. Floribundas were considered an improvement over hybrid teas because their bushes are hardier and more compact. However, although Floribundas are repeat-flowering, their abundant clusters of roses are considered a shortcoming from the one flower per stem perspective. The years that followed World War 2 saw an increased interest

Francis Meilland's "Mme A. Meilland" hybrid tea rose, 1935.

Lammerts's "Queen Elizabeth," Floribunda/ Grandiflora, 1954.

in the development of new roses. Each year for the past half century, a whole crop of new roses has appeared on the market. Grandiflora roses, for example, appeared in 1954. In the United States, Grandifloras hold the distinction of a separate class for rose shows and competitions. Elsewhere they are classified together with hybrid teas or Floribundas, as they are in fact a cross between the two, inheriting the best qualities from both sides. Grandifloras have the hybrid tea's long stems and single blooms, and the Floribunda's hardy bush with large, colorful, remontant flowers.

Beginning in the 1960s, the leading English rose grower David Austin brought things full circle by creating a gamut of modern roses with the look and fragrance* of old roses.* Called English roses,* they remain extremely popular.

Dwarf roses (apparently a favorite in imperial China) are not a new invention, however modern miniature roses almost all date from after World War II. They range in height from three to eighteen inches (7 to 45 cm), and although their flowers are perfectly formed, in most cases they are under a quarter of the normal size. Miniatures are perfect for planting in containers and small gardens. AE

Mutation

Like all living things, rosebushes can sometimes mutate. These mutations range from the invisible to the utterly spectacular. Mutations on the chromosomal level take place at the time of pollination or shortly after. They can affect any aspect of the rose, from coloring to fullness to fragrance.* These changes are sometimes the basis for new categories of roses, as in the case of the Moss Rose, a mutation of the *Rosa centifolia.*

A mutation, or "sport," can be apparent in one or several parts of a plant. Sports appear when suddenly a climbing branch appears on a shrub rose, or there is a single branch producing foliage or blooms of a different color from the rest of the bush. In the wild, mutations rarely survive and are soon overtaken by "normal" growth. An astute gardener, though, can detect an interesting sport and will try to propagate it by removing and grafting* it. Some cultivars, or rose groups, have a tendency to mutation, and there are a number of rose groups that have given rise to thirty or more varieties as a result of mutations. There can be no doubt that this element of surprise and novelty is part of what makes roses so fascinating. PB

THE NAME OF THE ROSE

After all the time and hard work it takes to create a new cultivar comes the difficulty of naming it. Breeders assign a series of numbers and letters to each rose at multiple points of its development in order to keep track of its lineage. If the resulting flower seems worthy of reproduction, it is named, again purely for administrative reasons. The name always begins with the first three letters of the breeding company. MEI for example stand for Meilland, DEL for Delbard, and AUS for Austin. This sometimes makes for rather unusual names, which nevertheless become the rose's fixed botanical designation. But the rose is also given another, far more evocative public name. Meivamo thus is called "Paris d'Yves Saint-Laurent," and Delpapy is dubbed "Souvenir de Marcel Proust."

In theory, the name is not translated and is the same in every country. But this rule is subject to exceptions depending on what a rose can spark off in the local imagination. The "Mme A. Meilland" rose is widely called the "Peace" rose in English-speaking nations, and "Gloria Dei" in Italy. "Iceberg" is a variety of "Fée des Neiges" (snow fairy) which is a translation into French of its German name, "Schneewittchen." An appealing name can actually be what lies behind a rose's popularity—and a dull, poorly chosen name can cause gardeners to turn up their noses at a rose that deserves better. There are no real rules governing the brand, commercial, or popular names for new roses. But it is, of course, a good policy to avoid names that may cause the new rose to be confused with existing or extinct roses, or other flowers. PB

Meilland's "Paris d'Yves Saint-Laurent," 1998.

Delbard's "Souvenir de Marcel Proust," 1993.

■ NEW ROSES AND OLD BUSHES

Most modern roses * are not hardy enough to produce a viable root system. Instead, they are budded or grafted* and grown on a stock or rootstock bush adapted to the targeted terrain and climate. When a rosebush is planted, the bud union (the point where the grafted part joins the rootstock) should be just about at level with the soil line. The branches above ground are now considered the rosebush, and the rootstock is buried. *Rosa canina* and *Rosa multiflora* are good rootstock choices.

It is not uncommon for growths to break through from the rootstock in spring and summer. These must be quickly done away with, or they will overtake the graft. The graft will also create new sprouts, and these should of course not be mistaken with those produced directly from the rootstock.

Faded flowers need to be cut off from repeat-flowering varieties and climbing roses to promote the second flowering. Selective pruning can also be used to control the volume of repeat-flowering rosebushes. Cutting is best done at the level of three or four leaves below the flower. With varieties that flower in large clusters, such as the Polyantha* and Floribuna* types, flowers should be nipped one by one, along with their buds, as soon as the petals fall. The branch can be cut later, after all the flowers have faded.

However, faded blooms should not be clipped on varieties that have decorative rose hips in the autumn. These include natural species,* spontaneous hybrid roses, and creepers. Bush and shrub roses that are not repeat-flowering can be pruned, but there is no need to rush to prune them as soon as the flowers fade. AE

Rosa rugosa.

Old Roses

A great number of rose varieties* and cultivars throughout the world can be loosely described as old or old-fashioned. Many of these roses are now quite hard to find; other varieties have been decimated by disease or frost, or through sheer neglect. Nevertheless, there are over ten thousand types of old-fashioned roses available on the market today.

The cut-off date which sets old roses off from their modern* counterparts is the year 1900. All old-fashioned varieties were already in existence before the turn of the nineteenth century, whereas nearly all modern roses were developed in the twentieth. The main difference between the two categories is based on appearance. With their characteristically stiff stems, modern roses can be even more beautiful as buds than as blooms, while the splendor of an old-fashioned rose comes in its blossoming. The old-fashioned rose's full-blown, often fragrant,* glory displays itself in a dazzling variety of sizes and shapes, including flat, convex, domed, and cup shaped. Old-fashioned roses come in subtle color gradations, ranging from white to deep scarlet, and from pink through mauve to dark crimson tones.

The term "old-fashioned" includes all indigenously occurring species* regardless of their country of origin, as well as the natural hybrids* that arise from spontaneous cross-pollination. These natural hybrids include such important varieties as the *Alba* and *Centifolia*, as well as Damask, Portland,* Bourbon,* and Tea* roses. All hybrids obtained from deliberate growers' crossbreeding of roses from among different families to create new groups are considered modern roses. An example of the latter hybrid is the crossing of the Noisette with the remontant (repeat-flowering) climbing hybrid which results in Tea rose hybrids.

The majority of the several thousand old-fashioned rose varieties currently in existence were carefully selected and developed by hybrid specialists throughout the course of the nineteenth century. Some contemporary rose breeders (notably the German grower Wilhelm Kordes and David Austin, father of the English rose) have produced modern varieties which resemble old-fashioned roses. AE

"Belle de Crécy" (*Rosa gallica*), 1848.

Old Versus New: Which to Choose?

The discovery of "La France," the first hybrid tea rose,* marked a century-long decline in interest in old and species roses. Just when it looked like modern roses* had carried the day, aficionados began finding fault with their new darlings. Suddenly these reigning favorites seemed too stiff, too artificial, too prone to disease. Old roses* became all the rage—a lucky reprieve, as some varieties had already disappeared, and others were on the point of extinction.

A modern rose in the old rose style: Meilland's "Concerto" Shrub rose, 1955.

Old roses are valued for their resistance to disease, intoxicating fragrance, and highly natural-looking spread and shrub forms. They can blend in with other plants, and are versatile in a garden. Many old roses which flower once a year produce bright rose hips in the fall. Modern roses are remontant, meaning they flower more than once, mainly in summer and in autumn. Their stems are often long, while their bushes are more compact. Modern roses typically have striking buds and long flowers on individual stems, though this is not the case for all varieties.

Choosing between old and new roses can be a question of space. For example, modern climbers tend to thin out more on the bottom as they develop toward the top, so an old climber might be preferred. If the roses are to live in a pot or container, miniature or other modern varieties could work best. But why choose? Contrary to popular opinion, there are plenty of repeat-flowering old roses, and a wide selection of fragrant moderns. In the final analysis, the question is more one of individual roses than of groups. In recent years the lines have been further blurred by the development of English roses,* pioneered in the 1960s by David Austin and other English specialists. English roses are designed to meld the best of old and new: their old-fashioned looking, heavily perfumed roses have semi-stiff stems and profuse repeat-flowering. English roses are disease-resistant and remain a favorite today. PB

A modern rose with an old rose look: Shepherd's "Golden Wings" hybrid, 1956.

PACKING

Rosebushes are sold packed in a variety of ways: bareroot; with their roots covered in peat moss; in containers; or in pots.

Bareroot roses are sold in a dormant state, without soil around their roots. They can be planted at any point during the non-growing season, November through April. Such plants must mature before being taken from the nursery for sale. The wood needs to have lived through autumn to be able to hold up in cold weather. Premature October planting* of young bushes is to be avoided.

The rosebushes often found for sale in stores and garden centers have roots protected by peat moss, which is kept in place by removable netting or string; the whole bush is then wrapped in plastic with a picture of the blossoming bush attached to a branch. This packing method allows for long storage without drying out the bush. An unintended side effect, however, is growth! It is important to avoid purchasing bushes that have already begun to sprout, since this early start makes the plant more susceptible to harsh winter weather.

Both bareroot and peat moss covered rosebushes should be very small and close to the root at the time of planting. Small size assures the concentration of the sap in the lowest branch nodes

Bareroot rosebush being planted.

and the grafting* point, which will become the areas of greatest strength in maturity.

Rosebushes sold in containers or pots allow for late planting in the spring and even summer, but the price is accordingly higher. These rosebushes are growing when sold, and are sometimes even in full bloom. Transplanting them in warm weather can be tricky business, especially if the plants have been forced* in a greenhouse to promote early flowering. The roots should have grown enough in the container to take hold in the soil, but they should not have coiled several times around in the pot. This indicates a plant two or three years old, one that will need a long time to adapt to new surroundings. AE

Paintings

The first known image of roses was discovered in 1900 by the British archeologist Arthur Evans at the Palace of Minos in Knossos, Crete. It dates from between 2000 and 1700 B.C.E., and is part of a decorative wall painting known as the *Bluebird Fresco*. The blossoms have bright orange centers and six golden petals, one more than the Phoenician rose that must have served as its model.

Medieval and Renaissance European artists used the rose to express religious and mythological themes alike. Especially fine Italian examples include: Stefano da Zevio's fifteenth-

century *Madonna in the Rosary*; the Annunciation paintings by Gentile de Fabriano and Lorenzo Salimbini in which the Archangel Gabriel is shown holding roses and lilies as he appears before the Virgin Mary; and Sandro Botticelli's *Birth of Venus*, in which the rose perfectly complements the goddess' beauty as she springs fresh from the waves.

Roses also appear in many portraits of Queen Elizabeth I (1533–1603), particularly eglantines, which she took as her personal flower. Other sixteenth-century English portraits also incorporate rose motifs, most notably in Nicholas

Filippo Lippi, *The Annunciation* (detail). Museo e Gallerie Nazionali di Capodimonte, Naples.

Hilliard's famous miniature, *Young man against a tree amongst the roses* (c. 1588).
In the seventeenth century, roses figured prominently in Flemish still life paintings, rendered with such precision that botanists today use them to identify old rose* varieties. Among those detected: *Rosa centifolia,* with its full cup shaped blooms, *Rosa* x *alba maxima, Rosa foetida,* and *Rosa moschatta* (the Musk rose). The great Flemish painters who did justice to the rose include the Brueghels, Jan Bosschaert, William van Aelst, and Jacob van Walscappelle, uncontested master of the genre.
There also exists a long tradition of botanical illustration, ranging from the miniatures of medieval Islam to the work of Pierre-Joseph Redouté, who between 1817 and 1824 assembled an invaluable record of the roses growing in the extensive gardens of the Empress Josephine.*

Patenting

Inventing a rose entails huge investments of time, money, talent, and technical know-how. It seems only fair that such an invention should be allowed to be patented in the same way that a new microchip component or an improved artificial sweetener would be. It may come as a surprise that there is considerable resistance to the granting of patents, and various ordinances throughout the world may effectively discourage agricultural specialists in their efforts. This is perhaps due to the idea that plants are living things, not subject to human order and authority. This unwillingness extends to the new and revived grains used to make breads and pasta, and even to the grapes used in winemaking.
A plant patent differs from a regular or "utility" patent because it relates to a living plant which cannot be "made" or "manufactured" in the same sense that an object can. A utility patent confers "the right to exclude others from making, using, or selling" an invention. Plant patents give "the right to exclude others from asexually reproducing the plant or selling or using the plant so reproduced, and parts thereof."
In the European Union, two years of testing and observation precede both the naming and the awarding of twenty-five year patents for new rose varieties. In the United States, plant patents only last twenty years, but this is an improvement over the 1997 conditions under which the patents were granted for seventeen years. PB

"I should like to know the true identity of this 'Madame Lauriol du Barny' who gave her name to such a sumptuous flower. I assume she must have belonged to the Haute cocotterie of Paris, or perhaps I am completely wrong and she was a perfectly respectable woman, the wife of a rose-grower from Lyons."

Vita Sackville-West

Rosebush being prepared for hybridizing, L'Haÿ-les Roses, France, c. 1900.

Rose water and soaps from Côté Bastide.

Perfume, Potions, and Potpourri

Of the more than ten thousand kinds of roses, only three are grown for use in making perfumes and cosmetics: the Cabbage rose (*Rosa centifolia*), the Damask rose (*Rosa damascena*) and the Tea rose *(Rosa indica)*. Throughout perfume history, the rose has been a star scent. Fragrance makers combine it with other aromas in a variety of ways to bring out spicy, peppery, fruity, or other characteristics.

Roses continue to be used in making cosmetics. Aside from providing fragrance, rose petals are astringent, and make a good skin toner. For countless centuries and throughout the world, rose water (see Attar of Roses) has been used in all sorts of beauty products, especially to soothe skin and improve its texture. Aromatherapy prizes the rose's fragrance for its soothing and regenerative effects, and the rose is a favored ingredient in this field.

Potpourri is thought to have originated with the Egyptian practice of burying the pharaohs with pots full of roses (potpourri means "rotten pot" in French). Now a traditional fragrance for the home, potpourri is easily made: simply gather up and save fallen rose petals. Other fragrant flowers such and lavender and violets may be added.

Meeting of Prince Humay and Princess Humayun in a Garden, c. 1450. Persian miniature, Musée des Arts décoratifs, Paris.

Persian Poetry

Born in Persia not long after the year 1000, the poet, philosopher, and mathematician Omar Khayyam wrote a long poem, the *Rubaiyat,* named after the rhyming quatrains in which it was written. Praising wine, women, and roses, its licentious attitude has outraged some and delighted a great many other readers, from Khayyam's time onwards. The eighteenth-century translation of the *Rubaiyat* by the Englishman Edward Fitzgerald is an impressive and acclaimed work in its own right, and certainly championed the cause of classical Persian poetry in Victorian England.

Khayyam wrote: "My tomb shall be in a spot where the north wind may scatter roses over it." Eager to see this spot, William Simpson of the *Illustrated London News* visited Naishápúr, where the poet had been laid to rest in 1122. He brought seeds of roses from the cemetery back to England, and they were planted in Kew Gardens. From these seeds grew the Damask rose which was appropriately named "Omar Khayyam." The rose first flowered in 1894, and a cutting from it was planted at Fitzgerald's grave at Boulge churchyard, near Woodbridge in Suffolk. In 1947, this historic rosebush was saved from death by Frank Knight. It is a low, upright shrub with very fragrant pale pink flowers.

Another of Persia's many literary rose lovers was Sa'adi, a poet and moralistof the thirteenth-century. It is said that Sa'adi was a slave who managed to pluck a rose at the very moment it was his turn to be sold. While still in chains he managed to bestow it upon a rich merchant with these words, "Be good to your servant for as long as you can, since time is as fleeting as the beauty of a rose." This earned him his freedom. Sa'adi was a mystic who saw the rose garden as a form of perfect ecstasy. All plants that grow alongside a rose take on its smell, said Sa'adi, manifest proof of the inter-relatedness of all things. His masterpiece is a work of ethics entitled *Gulistan* or *The Secret Rose Garden.* JB

Look to the blowing Rose about us—
"Lo, Laughing," she says,
"into the world I blow,
At once the silken tassel of my Purse Tear,
and its Treasure on the Garden throw."
"Wine! Wine! Wine! Red Wine!"—
the Nightingale cries to the Rose

from the Rubaiyat of Omar Khayyam,
(translated by Edward Fitzgerald)

■ PLANTING

The ideal planting time for roses depends on climate and the type of roses being used, but in general the best times are fall or early spring. Planting a hedge of roses takes a good deal of work. Rose bushes can grow in almost any kind of soil, as long as it is prepared the right way. There should be ample moisture in the subsoil, and it should be broken up to a depth of about two feet. Humus-forming material such as compost, chopped sod, or peat moss should be used to enrich the topsoil. Half a pound (186 g) of bone meal to each square yard (1 m) should also be added. Individual rosebushes can be set in holes fifteen inches (40 cm) wide, and deep enough to hold the roots. One common mistake is to plant roses too deep. The bottom soil has to be fertilized and packed down level to keep the bush balanced and upright. Fill the area around the root ball with fertile topsoil and pack it firmly, being careful not to break the roots. Add a mulch of hay, straw, leaves, or peat moss over the soil.

Rosebushes prefer rich, slightly acidic, well-packed soil. If the soil is heavy, it can be mixed with peat and some lighter soil. Avoid using compost for this, because it can cause rotting in the roots.

Bareroot rosebushes can be planted in the fall, if you live in a cooler climate, but only when there is little risk that temperatures will drop below freezing. In colder climates, early spring is the best time to plant. In the South, any time from mid-November to mid-February is fine. Those who have a choice might consider that roses planted in the spring usually don't start growing as vigorously or as soon as those that are planted in the fall. The roots should be lightly cut back all around the ends with a clean cut. The branches should be pruned down to four inches (10 cm) from the grafting* point, keeping only the three or four strongest and best placed branches; only two or three branches for climbing roses. This drastic pruning will make for strong, solid growth.

If the weather is dry at the time of planting, water the bushes immediately. Later, when the soil is dry, check the bushes to make sure that they are firmly planted. If they can be moved even the slightest bit, pack them in more firmly. Spread a mound of soil or peat moss over the base of the branches six to eight inches high.

Rosebushes sold packed* in peat moss should be planted without removing the peat. First soak it in water for at least an hour. Forced* rosebushes sold in containers in the spring have delicate foliage unused to soil and susceptible to heat. It is good to plant these on an overcast day that will be followed by more overcast weather. If that is not possible, cover the plants with an umbrella or improvised shade for the first few days. AE

Bareroot rosebush.

Sugaring the roots.

Planting.

Rosa polyantha shrub in flower.

Polyantha

Polyanthas are sometimes called Baby Ramblers. *Rosa polyantha* date to the nineteenth century, and derive from crossing *Rosa multiflora* with the Chinese* rose "Old* Blush China." The stout shrubs grow low and hardy. The small flowers bloom in large clusters, and last long when they are cut. A Polyantha can continue flowering all summer long. PB

Portland Roses

The origin of the Portland rose is still a matter of debate. It is a hybrid of the Autumn Damask* and *Rosa gallica* "Officinalis," and is known to have existed as far back as 1792. The rose is named for Margaret Cavendish Bentinck, second Duchess of Portland. She found one of its ancestors growing in Italy and brought seeds to England where she cultivated it. André Dupont, Descenet's successor

at Malmaison,* also cultivated a plant provided by the duchess. The Portland rosebush is small and shrubby. The flowers are full and repeat bloom in summer and autumn. The Portland rose was intensively bred in the nineteenth century, and gave rise to over eighty varieties. Today the Portland is no longer quite so fashionable, but some varieties are still going strong. These are true, highly fragrant,* old-fashioned roses. PB

■ PRUNING

Pruning stimulates the formation and growth of strong new shoots on a rosebush. It also prevents the spread of disease* and allows the plant to be kept in a pleasing shape.

Bush, shrub, and climbing roses are all pruned differently. The most common roses in gardens today are hedge-type Polyanthas* and Floribundas.* These are modern roses* bred for abundant repeat-flowering. They should be pruned back sharply in the early spring. Make room around the central area of the plant, while preserving young, healthy-looking branches. Pruning should also be done after summer flowering.

Repeat-flowering rosebushes should be pruned just before the leaves fall for winter. Cut back new branches and remove dying or dead old ones to give the center air. The plant can also be shaped. Rosebushes that flower only once should be pruned once the flowers are gone, which is usually by mid-summer.

Climbing roses should be trained on trellises. After they flower, cut back the side branches by half their length. Selectively remove old branches to favor new growth. Dead wood and branches can be cleared away from single flowering and climbing roses in the course of the summer. Prune any branches that re-flowered in the autumn, and cut away all dead and dying branches in winter. AE

Rambling Roses

Rambling and climbing roses do just as their names suggests. These roses break down into three main groups: ramblers, climbers, and large-flowered climbers. But there is a lot of overlap since many types of roses can be trained to climb. Many varieties of ramblers were developed in the early twentieth century by crossing with *Rosa wichuraiana.* This species is a native of Japan, Korea, and China. It grows mainly along the coast, where it flourishes over dunes and rocks. With ancestors like that, rambling

roses are obviously quite hardy. Some varieties have shoots that can grow up to fifteen inches (40 cm) in a year. Ramblers were at one time very popular, but have long since been eclipsed by the fashion for large-flowered climbers.

The category of climbing roses is broad enough to include a range of roses that easily adapt to climbing habits, including hybrid teas, Teas,* Polyanthas* and Floribundas.* Climbing varieties of these rosebushes come from mutations* of bush varieties which were brought out through breeding.

REPLACEMENT

The life span of a rosebush is hard to guess. There are some gardens with rosebushes that are more than a hundred years old, with center branches wide as tree trunks and no sign of quitting. Yet other plants die suddenly after a year or two of healthy existence. The gardener has one simple golden rule: when a plant is ailing or dead it must be pulled out and replaced.

When a single shrub in a bed or hedgerow needs replacing, it can be done in early autumn. A new rosebush among old ones won't necessarily have an easy time adapting, and requires careful attention. The soil where the previous plant was should be removed

to a depth of at least eighteen inches (40 to 50 cm) and replaced with fresh topsoil. If the bed was comprised of mixed varieties, make sure the new plants balance the old ones in hardiness and growth capacity. Potted plants can be used to replace young rosebushes over the course of the summer.

If an entire hedgerow or rose bed needs replacing, the whole area must be dug out, and the soil removed eighteen inches (45 cm) down. Break up and renew the subsoil and add a loamy topsoil. The next best solution is to give the earth a chance to renew itself for a few seasons by growing other kinds of flowers in its place. AE

Guillaume de Lorris and Jean de Meun, *Roman de la Rose*, c. 1460. Bibliothèque Nationale de France, Paris.

Romaunt of the Rose

The rose—symbol of purity, symbol of love—is the central subject of the extremely influential medieval allegory, the *Roman de la Rose*. Like a hybrid* or remontant rosebush whose flowering takes place twice annually, the first quarter of this French poem was written by Guillaume de Lorris in about 1235 and the remainder was executed by Jean de Meun some forty-five years later.

The first part of poem is a dream-vision, in which a young aristocrat seeks a mystic union with his lady (represented as a rose) and strives to protect her against a host of allegorical enemies such as Hate, Age, Jealousy, and Greed. The poem's continuation moves beyond courtly romance into satire, providing ironic commentary on the social issues of the day.

An English version (*Romaunt of the Rose*) appeared towards the end of the fourteenth century,

allegedly translated by Geoffrey Chaucer. Traces of characters such as the Old Woman appear in Chaucer's masterpiece, *The Canterbury Tales.* JB

Rome

Roses appear in Minoan wall paintings, and it is clear that the ancient Greeks knew them as well. But it is the Romans who left the most evidence of their enthusiasm for and cultivation of roses. They grew several species* and varieties; a favorite was the white *Rosa* x *alba,* which still blooms today.

Roses were a status symbol, and any self-respecting patrician had to have a rose garden. To impress and woo the great Marc Antony, Cleopatra received him in chambers piled high in rose petals. The Emperor Heliogabalus (204–224 C.E.) sprinkled such an abundance of rose petals for his coronation festivities that several of his guests died from suffocation.

The Romans wore crowns of roses at feasts and social occasions, and used them to make perfumes, cosmetics, and potions, both medicinal and magical. For banquets, they strewed the floors with rose petals and floated them in their wine. Rose crowns were worn at orgies to ward against the unwanted side effects of drinking. Brides and grooms were decorated with roses, as were images of Venus and Cupid. Roses were strewn everywhere for the feasts of Flora and Hymen: in the paths of victors,

Lawrence Alma-Tadema, *The Roses of Heliogabalus.* Private collection, Paris.

beneath chariot-wheels, and on the prows of battleships. The rose was also central to the festival of *Rosalia* in May and June, when the tombs of dead relatives were decorated with roses, and rose petals were offered up to the dead spirits. So great was the call for roses that several large horticultural centers were set up for intensive growing. Forcing* and irrigation with thermal spring water were used. Even this did not satisfy demand, and petals had to be shipped in from Carthage and Egypt. PB

Rosary

The word rosary comes from the Latin term *rosarium,* which refers to both the crowns of roses placed on statues of the Virgin Mary, and a rose garden. According to legend, Mary gave Saint Dominique a rose which had bloomed on Christ's crown of thorns, and asked him to gather roses so the first ceremony of the rosary could be performed. This bouquet, along with the practice of repeating certain associated prayers, evolved into the rosary as we now know it. And although today's rosaries are made from a variety of materials, early strands sometimes used beads made from dried rose petals and perfumed with attar of roses.* JB

Rose Window

The magnificent round windows set high in the transepts of Gothic cathedrals are in fact roses, stylized and enlarged to enormous proportions. The rose windows of Notre-Dame in Paris, for example, are almost forty-three feet (thirteen meters) in diameter.

Important too is the religious symbolism of these astonishing "blossoms." For Christians, the

Caravaggio, *Madonna of the Rosary,* 1606–07. Kunsthistorisches Museum, Vienna.

Alsatian School, *Rose Window from the Eastern Façade of Strasbourg Cathedral* (detail), c. 1380. Musée de l'Oeuvre de Notre-Dame, Strasbourg.

Antonio Canova, *Venus Crowning Adonis,* 1789. Canova Museum, Possagno.

seven-petaled rose recalls the seven days of creation in the Bible as well as Christ's seven wounds on the cross. It is also a sign of resurrection and immortal life.

Their round shape also associates rose windows with other symbolic possibilities—the sun, the world, the fullness and fleetingness of life, and the turning of Fortune's wheel. JB

The Dragon of Chaos. Paris, Bibliothèque Nationale de la France

Secrecy

According to mythology, Venus gave her son Eros a rose and asked him to bring it to Harpocrates, the god of silence, so that her affairs of the heart would remain secret. This story was the source of the Roman* custom of hanging a rose from the ceiling when those present at a gathering were to be asked to hold their tongues about the matter. The expression *sub rosa,* which literally means "under the rose" in Latin, comes from this practice, and the rose-shaped moldings which decorates the ceilings in many older buildings may also well be an echo of the ancient tradition. During World War II, the insignia of British intelligence officers was a rose with the word "intelligence" written on it, and this too may relate to the idea of *sub rosa.* JB

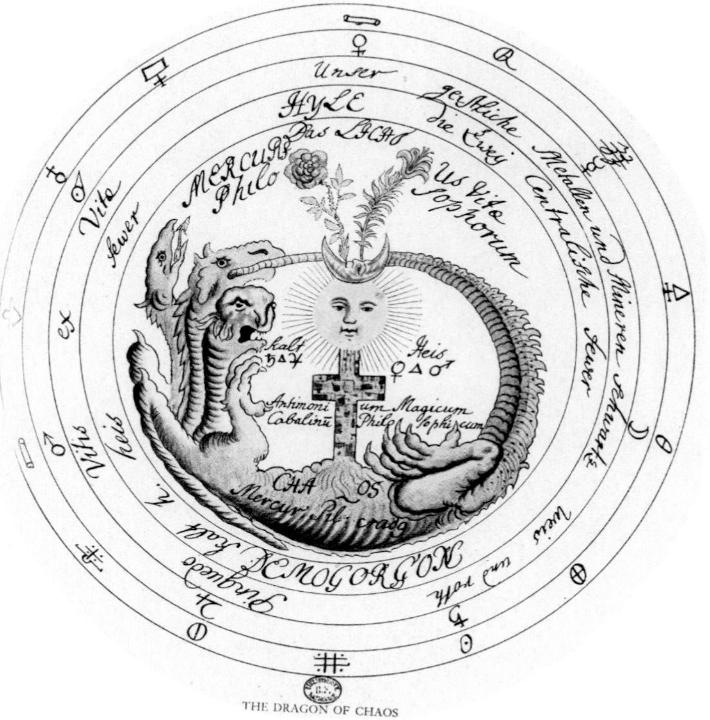

THE DRAGON OF CHAOS

ADONE INGHIRLANDATO
DA VENERE ED AMORINO

■ SELECTING ROSES

From wild roses* to the latest modern creations, catalogues offer several hundred varieties of roses to choose from. The array can be mind-boggling for first-timers and seasoned gardeners alike, and decisions are often made based on the illustrations alone. The best policy is to visit gardens during growing season and make notes on the different varieties' characteristics and their compatibility with other plants. Each garden is a special case, and the rosebush must be able to adapt to its placement. Color and personal taste are important considerations, but the overall harmony* of the garden must be kept in mind at all times.

Modern roses* are most often grown in separate beds rather than mixed in with other flowers. They are almost always repeat-flowering, with a primary blossoming in May or June (depending on climate), and a second blooming in September or October. The abundance of the second flowering varies according to the species,* climatic conditions, and care* during the summer months. There is a wide range of species* and old rose* shrubs. They may flower only once yearly but the single May or June blossoming can be truly spectacular. The flowering is often followed by the production of rose hips in the fall for two to three months. These rosebushes are true hedges and can cover a great expanse of ground in a garden. A climbing rose may be selected for a garden with walls or other suitable surfaces. As a rosebush extends upward, its lower growth becomes increasingly sparser, so less high-reaching varieties of climbers may eventually need to be added to fill in at the bottom. AE

Field of rose beds grown for Meilland, Le Luc-en-Provence, France.

Thorns of a *Rosa sericea*. f. *pteracantha*, 1890.

Sowing

Once a new rose has been hybridized* the seeds have to be planted for a new rosebush to grow.

Rose hips ripen in the fall, and are crushed to remove the seeds. They are either exposed to cold or washed to destroy the protective coating that keeps them from germinating. The seeds are then sown in covered beds of light soil. The area is not heated, except in cases of extreme cold, because heat keeps seeds from germinating. Rose plants may blossom as soon as three months after germination. However, the first flowers are not necessarily characteristic of what the mature rosebush will produce. The young transplants initially only indicate such factors as shape, repeat-flowering abilities, and hardiness over time.

Three to four thousand plants out of the sixty thousand sown every year make it past the stage when experts judge them in every category, from shrub appearance to fragrance. Once a new rosebush has been propagated by grafting,* samples are sent out for trial growth around the world, and all the relative merits are again subject to expert scrutiny. In a good year, only five or six rosebushes out of the original sixty thousand seedlings are still in the running at this point, while in an off year the number may be zero. Once officially named,* the winners go on to compete for favor in the public eye and at flower shows.* PB

Species

Species are constituted by both roses found growing naturally in their original habitats (whether the Near or Middle East, Asia, North America, or Europe) and the natural hybrid* varieties that result from spontaneous cross-breeding. In their places of origin, such roses multiplied over the centuries to cover both mountains and plains.

Georges Bugnet's "Thérèse Bugnet" *Rosa rugosa* hybrid, 1950.

Some varieties were first brought to Europe by medieval crusaders. Others were brought over by eighteenth and nineteenth-century missionaries and merchants. It was during this period that European botanists worked to develop a horticultural classification* system for rose species based on botanical criteria. This system is constantly being modified and improved, because of advances made in terms of chemical and color analysis, for instance.

All roses grow as bushes, whether large or small. Branches can extend to great lengths, and all have thorns. The thorns may be sliver-thin (*Rosa rugosa*), broad (*Rosa sericea.* f. *pteracantha*), or barely discernible (*Rosa banksiae*). Flowers consist of five petals, five sepals, and inferior or epigynous ovaries located beneath the petals. The leaves are comprised of three to nine sections. Flowers blossom on the lateral branches which grow from the wood of the preceding year. Some roses produce berry-like rose hips that are highly decorative in appearance. PB

Spontaneous Crossbreeds

The earth is a good mother, says one adage. Rose-lovers might agree. Without any help from humans, nature has hybridized* roses in abundance. Hundreds of types of roses that were thought to have been pure species* have recently been proven to be the result of cross-pollination, aided by busy birds and bees and other insects. With few exceptions, most notably the Damask rose,* these roses thrive mainly in the wild* and are not directly used in gardens.*

There are also many cases of crossbreeding where civilization played an accidental role. Back when Réunion Island was known as Bourbon Island, hedges of roses were planted as barriers. As a result the "Old Blush" China rose, which is repeat-flowering but on the delicate side, spontaneously crossed with the Damask "Semperflorens," which is fragrant and hardy with double flowers that tend not to repeat flower. This gave birth to the beloved Bourbon* rose in the early nineteenth century. Horticulturists have sought to imitate this process by mixing a number of varieties* and cultivars in the same planting area, and sowing the seeds that result. The rosebushes that come from these experiments are often replicas of preexisting cultivars. PB

Tea Roses

The first Tea rose was created in 1835 in England. It was the result of successive crossings of the China* roses "Hume's Blush" tea-scented China, and "Parks' Yellow" tea-scented China, with Bourbon* and Noisette varieties.

Tea roses proved important in rose history by giving rise to the hybrid tea rose,* the best-known of all modern roses.* But the original Tea roses are old, full-bodied shrubs that are relatively delicate and fare best in mild climates.

Hybrid tea roses are a blend of Tea roses and repeat-flowering hybrid varieties. The first hybrid teas can be traced back to 1859. Hybrid tea roses grow on rather stiff shrubs. They have elongated buds, flower abundantly throughout the summer, and are highly fragrant.* PB

Meilland's "Galia," hybrid tea rose, 1978.

Henry Payne, *The Legend of the War of the Roses.* City Museum and Art Gallery, Birmingham.

War of the Roses

More than any other flower, the roses have been as an emblem for warriors and armies. Achilles had one on his shield, Roman soldiers wore them into battle, crusaders bore them back from the Holy Land, and—most famously—they gave their name to the War of the Roses.

In the mid-fifteenth century, a dispute between the houses of York and Lancaster began thirty years of war. Each side bore a rose as its symbol: the Yorks used *Rosa* x *alba* , now known as the White Rose* of York, while the Lancasters bore the red-colored Apothecary Rose, *Rosa gallica officinalis.* Legend has it that the two families stopped feuding when a rosebush was found in the British countryside that had flowers of both colors. The "York and Lancaster" or "Tudor Rose" was long thought to be this fabled rose of red and white, but in fact was not introduced until 1551. The bloodshed and fratricide actually came to an end in 1485, with Henry VII of Lancaster's marriage to Elizabeth of York. Their union founded the royal House of Tudor, whose most illustrious monarch, Elizabeth I, often incorporated roses into her devices and emblems.

Today, the rose is still a royal and patriotic symbol in England. It can be found in the insignia of honors such as the Order of the Garter and the Order of Bath. And a red rose on a white background is even worn by England's national rugby team! JB

"And here I prophesy: this brawl to-day, grown to this faction in the Temple-garden, shall send between the red rose and the white, a thousand should to death and deadly night."

William Shakespeare, Henry VI, Part I, II.iv.123-126

White or Red?

While roses now come in all hues, from the darkest purple to the lightest yellow, red and white have always been the most symbolic colors of the rose.

In the last lines of the *Divine Comedy*, Dante, with Beatrice as his guide, has a vision of the "Mystic Rose." This is a white rose, *Rosa candida,* for Christians a symbol of pure, divine love. For Dante it was "the rose in which the Word is made Flesh." Yet the very thought of incarnation brings an image of reddening, like blood quickening in the veins.

According to one legend, the first white rose was born of the drops of sweat shed by the Prophet Mohammed. Another tradition holds that the white rose came from sea foam, just like Aphrodite, the Greek goddess of love and beauty. But the red rose is also attributed to Aphrodite. It is said to have been colored by the blood of the goddess when she was wounded by the thorns that separated her from her mortal lover, Adonis. In Eastern lore, the red rose symbolizes the blissful smile of sated lovers, while according to Christian mystics, it was seen to bloom over Christ's body in his agony.

A hauntingly beautiful legend about origin of red roses is told in India. Wanting to delight lovers all night long with its magical singing, a nightingale pressed its breast against a snow-white rose in order to stay awake. As the bird's blood slowly stained the pale flowers, the first red rose was created.

Which came first, the white rose or the red? This unanswerable question is like asking which was first imagined: heaven or hell, good or evil, light or dark. Opposites attract and all distinctions blur, as Rainer Marie Rilke wrote: "Rose, oh pure contradiction."

WILD ROSES AND DOG ROSES

In an earlier era, when taste in roses favored a more opulent style, wild and dog rosebushes were valued mainly as stock for grafting* or, more infrequently, for hybrids.* Today these roses are appreciated for their own fresh-looking, simple blooms, fine foliage, and yield of highly decorative rose hips in the fall.

Rosa x *alba* is quite possibly the very rose beloved by the ancient Romans.* This very old natural hybrid has white semi-double or double flowers which blossom in June, according to climate. It is of average height, with matte leaves. Other popular wild roses include *Rosa banksiae,* especially in its fairly hardy "Lutea" form. In the garden of La Mortola in Italy this climbing rose has been reported to reach up to 200 feet (60 m) in length. It will blossom after its second or third year, and its mellow yellow clusters give off a light scent when they flower in June or July. This rose is on the delicate side, and is not viable for cold climates, as the bushes need to be covered in mulch and straw to survive the winter, even in mild climates. *Rosa moschata* is admired for its incomparable scent. The "Autumnalis" form flowers very late, in August or even September. Its subdued beauty is best offset when the shrub is planted amid brightly colored perennials.

Dog rose (*Rosa canina*).

Wild roses exist in a variety of colors. The hardy *Rosa californica* "Plena" bursts into tufted bunches of deep pink flowers, weighing down the branches in elegant arches. *Rosa chinensis* "Mutabilis" is a striking cultivar whose buds open with a beige yellow tone which ripens to pink and finally deep crimson when full-blown. Young leaves are a beautiful translucent crimson. This rose hates the cold, but can flourish in southern regions, bearing flowers up to ten months out of the year. The *Rosa foetida,* also known as the Austrian Brier or Austrian Yellow, displays an abundance of brilliant yellow blooms in June. Its cultivar "Bicolor," the Austrian Copper, has been known since the twelfth century and probably originated in Turkey. Its petals are yellow in the center and on the reverse side, but red on the inside. The unique *Rosa glauca* is loved for its graceful foliage which is a deep red with blue tints. This unusual coloration perfectly compliments the deep pink of the small flowers with their white centers. The *Rosa glauca* spreads like a raspberry bush. The flowers of *Rosa nitida* are not showy, but the shrub has bright leaves that turn a dazzling coppery color in the fall.

Last but not least comes *Rosa rugosa,* whose crimson, pink, or white flowers are highly fragrant and partially repeat-flowering. This rose can hold its own against salty sea air, harsh winds, and even pollution. PB

Walter Crane, *Portrait of Mary Frances Crane,* 1882. Musée d'Orsay, Paris

MARY · FRANCES · CRANE

Everlasting yellow roses.

Yellow Rose of Texas

"The Yellow Rose of Texas" is the state song of Texas, as well as a traditional American favorite. The tune and the tale seems straightforward enough, but a little scratching at the surface uncovers the romantic mystery and uncertainty that is part of all good rose stories.

The song's original version, first written down in 1836, tells of an African-American man separated from his sweetheart and longing to return to her. It is assumed that he was a soldier fighting in the war for the independence of Texas from Mexico, which took place at that time. "Yellow" was a term used for a particular light black or mulatto skin tone. The song was the hit of its time. Originally, the first verse and chorus went:

There's a yellow rose in Texas,
that I am going to see,
No other darky knows her,
no darky only me
She cried so when I left her it
like to broke my heart,
And if I ever find her,
we nevermore will part.
[Chorus]
She's the sweetest rose of color
this darky ever knew,
Her eyes are bright as diamonds,
they sparkle like the dew;
You may talk about your Dearest
May, and sing of Rosa Lee,
But the Yellow Rose of Texas
beats the belles of Tennessee.

During the Civil War, this song became a soldiers' marching

tune, particularly for Texan troops. The lyrics were changed, with the word "darky" replaced by "soldier," and "rose of color" becoming "little flower."

The song's original title, "Emily, the Maid of Morgan's Point," and the accompanying legend, suggest that the yellow Rose of Texas may have been a woman named Emily Morgan. Emily Morgan was an indentured servant in the household of James Morgan, a Philadelphia slaveholder who resettled in Texas in 1830. Because slavery was illegal in Texas, Morgan changed the status of his slaves to ninety-nine year indentured servants. Morgan became a colonel in the Texan army, and left his hacienda to fight. The Mexican commander General Santa Anna pillaged Morgan's property and took Emily Morgan and a young boy among his spoils. Emily supposedly sent the boy to find the Texan hero Sam Houston to lead him to Santa Anna. In the meanwhile, she determined to entrap the Mexican general with her beauty. When the Texan troops arrived, Santa Anna's attentions were engaged by the beautiful woman, and his forces were defeated in the ensuing battle.

It is said that James Morgan was so pleased with his slave's patriotism that he freed her. Whether or not this is so, he went on to tell the story of her exploits for years to come—including to the English ethnologist William Bollaert, who recorded the story in detail.

Although it is improbable that the "Yellow Rose of Texas" has any relation to a particular flower, there has been much speculation over just which rose this yellow rose may have been. Some claim it is *Rosa x. harisonii* or "'Harison's Yellow," a crossbreed of *Rosa foetida persiana* ("Persian Yellow") with *Rosa pimpinellifolia* ("Scotch Briar").

David Austin's "Graham Thomas" English Rose, 1983.

B U Y E R ' S

ROSE NURSERIES

UNITED STATES
Antique Rose Emporium Rte 5
P.O. Box 143
Brenham, TX 77833
Tel.: (409) 836-9051

Chamblee's Roses
10926 U.S. Hwy
69 NorthTyler
TX 75706-8742
Tel.: (903) 882-3597

Heirloom Roses
24062 NE Riverside Drive
St. Paul, OR 97137
Tel.: (503) 538-1576

Historical Roses
1657 West Jackson Street
Painesville, OH 44077
Tel.: (440) 357-7270

Mendocino Heirloom Roses
P.O. Box 670
Mendocino, CA 95460
Tel.: (707) 937-0963

Muncy's Rose Emporium
11207 Celestine Pass
Sarasota, FL 34240
Tel.: (941) 377-6156

CANADA
Hardy Roses for the North
P.O. Box 2048
Grand Forks, BC V0H 1H0
Tel.: (604) 442-8442

Mockingbird Lane Roses
4464 Clarke Road,
Port Burwell, Ontario N0J 1TO
Tel.: (519) 874-4811

GREAT BRITAIN
Cants of Colchester Ltd
Nayland Road, Mile End
Colchester, Essex CO4 5EB
Tel.: 01206 844 008

David Austin Roses
Bowling Green Lane
Albrighton,
Nr Wolverhampton WV7
Tel.: 01902 37391

Dickson Nurseries Ltd
Milecross Road
Newtonards, Co Down BT23 4SS
Tel.: 02891 812 206

R. Harkness & Co Ltd
Cambridge Road
Hitchin,
Herts SG4 0JT
Tel.: 01462 420 402

John Sanday Ltd
Over Lane
Almondsbury,
Bristol BS12 4DA

Peter Beales Roses
London Road,
Attleborough,
Norfolk NR17 1AY
Tel.: 01953 424 707

Trevor White Old
Fashioned Roses
Bennett's Brier
The Street, Felthorpe
Norfolk NR10 4AB
Tel.: (01603 755135

AUSTRALIA
Remontant Roses
600 East Kurrajong Road
Kurrajong East,
NSW 2758
Tel.: (2) 4576 5256

Ross Roses
Saint Andrews
Willunga,
SA 5172
Tel.: (8) 8556 2555

Showtime Roses
20, Abbin Avenue
Bentleigh East,
VIC 3165
Tel.: (3) 9557 6144

FRANCE
André Ève
Morailles
BP 206
45302 Pithiviers-le-Vieil
Tel : 02 38 30 01 30

Delbard
16, quai de la Mégisserie
75001 Paris
Tel : 01 44 80 20 20

Meilland Richardier
50, rue Deperet
69160 Tassin La Demi-Lune
Tel : 04 78 34 46 52

ROSE SOCIETIES

AMERICAN ROSE SOCIETY
P.O. Box 30,000
Shreveport, LA 71130-0030
Tel.: (318) 938-5402
Fax: (318) 938-5405
Email: ars@ars-hq.org
www.ars.org

HERITAGE ROSE FOUNDATION
1512 Gorman Street
Raleigh, NC 27606
Tel.: (919) 834-2591
Email: rosefoun@aol.com

CANADIAN ROSE SOCIETY
17 Kintyre Avenue
Toronto
Ontario M4L M2
Tel.: (416)466 1879
www.mirror.org/group/crs

ROYAL NATIONAL ROSE SOCIET
The Gardens of the Rose
Chiswell Green
Saint Albans
Herts AL2 3NR
Tel.: (01727) 850461
Email: mail@rnrs.org.uk
www.roses.co.uk

NATIONAL ROSE SOCIETY OF AUSTRALIA
29 Columbia Crescent
Modbury North, SA 5092
Australia
Tel.: (08) 8264 0084

THE ROSE SOCIETY OF NORTHE IRELAND
15 Carnduff Road
Larne,
Co. Antrim BT40 3NJ
Tel.: (02828) 272658
E-mail: info@rosemerald.co.uk

Société Française des Roses
Roseraie du Parc de la Tête d'O
69006 Lyon
Tel.: 04 74 94 04 36

GUIDE

ROSE GARDENS

United States

Los Angeles Arboretum
301 North Baldwin Avenue
Arcadia, CA 91007-2697
Tel.: (626) 821-3222

Berkeley Rose Garden
1201 Euclid Ave
Berkeley, CA 94708
Tel.: (415) 644-6530

Elizabeth Park Rose Garden
150 Walbridge Road
West Hartford, CT 06119
Tel.: (860) 242-0017

Longue Vue Gardens
7 Bamboo Road
New Orleans,
LA 70124-1065
Tel.: (504) 488-5488

Hampton Historic Site
535 Hampton Lane
Towson, MD 21286
Tel.: (410) 962-0688

Governor Langdon Mansion
143 Pleasant Street
Portsmouth, NH 03801
Tel.: (603) 436-3205

Clark Botanic Garden
193 I. U. Willets Road
Albertson, NY 11507
Tel.: (516) 484-8600

New York Botanical Garden
200th Street
Bronx, New York,
NY 10458
Tel.: (718) 817-8700

National Herb Garden
U.S. National Arboretum
3501 New York Avenue NE
Washington,
DC 20002
Tel.: (202) 472-9259

Washington National
Cathedral Gardens
Wisconsin Avenue NW,
Washington,
DC 20016-5098
Tel.: (202) 537-2937

Canada

Centennial Rose Garden
Dogwood Pavilion
621 Poirier St., Coquitlam BC

Jardin Botanique de Montréal
4101 Sherbrooke St. E.
Montreal,
Quebec H1X 2B2
Tel.: (514) 872-1400

Royal Botanical Gardens
680 Plains Road West
Burlington, Ontario

Great Britain

Royal National Rose Society
Chiswell Green Lane
Saint Albans,
Herts AL2 3NR
Tel.: (01727) 850461

Mottisfont Abbey Garden
Romsey,
Hampshire S051 0LJ
Tel.: (01794) 340757

Royal Botanic Gardens, Kew
Richmond,
Surrey TW9 3AVB
Tel.: (0208) 940 1171

Sissinghurst Castle
Sissinghurst, Cranbrook,
Kent TN17 2AB
Tel.: (01580) 710701

Sudeley Castle
Winchcombe, Cheltenham,
Gloucestershire GL54 5JD
Tel.: (01242) 602308

Australia

National Botanic Gardens
GPO Box 1777
Canberra, ACT 2601
Tel.: (02) 62509450

France

Hôtel Baudy
Musée-Restaurant
81, rue Claude Monet,
27620 Giverny
Tel.: 02 32 21 10 03

Roseraie du Val-de-Marne
8, rue Albert Watel
94240 L'Haÿ-les-Roses
Tel.: 01 43 99 82 80

SELECTED BIBLIOGRAPHY

Austin, David. *David Austin's English Roses.* Boston: Little, Brown and Company, 1993.

Druitt, Liz. *The Organic Rose Garden.* Dallas: Taylor Publishing Co., 1996.

Girard-Lagorce, Sylvie. *The Book of Roses.* Paris: Flammarion, 2000.

Griffiths, Trevor. *The Book of Old Roses.* London: Michael Joseph, 1983.

Le Rougetel, Hazel. *A Heritage of Old Roses.* London: Unwin Hyman, 1988.

Macoboy, Stirling. *The Ultimate Rose Book.* New York: Harry N. Abrams, Inc., 1993.

Ohrbach, Barbara. *Roses for the Scented Room.* New York: Clarkson Potter, 2000.

Phillips, Rodger, and Martyn Rix. *The Random House Guide to Roses.* New York: Random House, 1988.

Reddell, Rayford C. *The Rose Bible.* New York: Harmony Press, 1994.

I N D E X

INDEX

Photographic credits: Authors' archives 26; Meilland 32, 75, 106; NEUILLY, Photothèque des Amis des Jardins 42 top, 60, 96–97 /P. Fernandes 4–5, 22–23, 47 top, 62 top, 48–49, 80-81, 66-67, 50–51, 57, 76–77 bottom, 64 left, 64 middle, 64 right, 44–45, 45 bottom, 89 left, 37 right, 37 left /P. Ferret 13, 21, 54–55, 62 bottom, 53 bottom, 89 top, 92–93 /J. Le Bret 78, 89 left, 89 right /P. Poupart 77 right /J.F. Jarreau 70 ; LONDON, Bridgeman Art Library 24, 110; PARIS, Bibliothèque nationale de France 33, 98, 102 bottom; Philippe Bonduel 43, 28, 29, 91 bottom, 79 bottom, 79 top; Dagli Orti, 38–39, 52, 82–83, 40, 103; © cliché Delbard 75; Jacana/Y. Delange 14–15 /Ruffier-Lanche 104–105 /J.P. Soulier 42 bottom /J.P. Thomas 66–67 /M. Viard 58–59 /D. Lecourt 73, 74 /C. Nardin 90–91 /É. Chanvril 37 left /C. Favardin 47, 37 top, 109; Chris Kutchera 27, 17; Magnum/Erich Lessing 25, 61, 100; Réunion des musées nationaux 68, 113, 30, 65; Roger-Viollet 84 Rustica 53; PITHIVIERS, André Ève 12 left, 12 right, 47, 69; VANVES, Explorer 46, 107, 48–49 112, 94–95; Gamma 41; Giraudon 10, 20, 101 /Lauros-Giraudon 72 /Bridgeman-Giraudon 98–99.

Translated and adapted from the French by Chet Wiener and Stacey Doris
Copy-editing: Kathryn Lancaster
Typesetting: Claude-Olivier Four
Color separation: Pollina S.A., France

Originally published as *L'ABCdaire de la rose* © 1996 Flammarion
English-language edition © 2002 Flammarion

ISBN: 2-0801-0675-9
N° d'édition: FA0675-01-XI
Dépôt légal: 3/2002
Printed and bound by Pollina S.A, France - n° L84965

pp. 4–5: Rose Garden, Parc de Bagatelle, Paris.